THE 'CLIO'

THE 'CLIO'

1877–1920

A STUDY OF THE FUNCTIONS OF AN
INDUSTRIAL TRAINING SHIP IN NORTH WALES

by
Emrys Wyn Roberts

First published in 2011

© Emrys Wyn Roberts

ISBN: 978-184524-180-3

Cover design: Lynwen Jones

Published by
Llygad Gwalch, Ysgubor Plas, Llwyndyrys,
Pwllheli, Gwynedd, Wales, LL53 6NG.
Tel: 01758 750432
e-mail: books@carreg-gwalch.com
www.carreg-gwalch.com

Dedicated to Harri Wyn

Contents

		Page
Contents		7
Acknowledgements		8
Summary		9
CHAPTER 1	Introduction	10
CHAPTER 2	The establishment of industrial training ships	16
CHAPTER 3	Establishing the I.T.S. Clio	23
CHAPTER 4	Conditions under which boys could be sent to the Clio	43
CHAPTER 5	The rules and by-laws regulating the constitution and management of the society governing the I.T.S. Clio	48
CHAPTER 6	1878 – The first year and teething troubles	73
CHAPTER 7	Daily routine on board the Clio	77
CHAPTER 8	School time-table and curriculum	84
CHAPTER 9	Training for the sea	103
CHAPTER 10	Life on the 'Clio' 1879-1890	110
CHAPTER 11	Problems with the code of 1895, and the difficulty of obtaining boys	127
CHAPTER 12	A new century – a new captain	134
CHAPTER 13	Tragedy strikes	143
CHAPTER 14	1907 until the outbreak of the First World War	158
CHAPTER 15	The First World War and the end of the Clio	163
CHAPTER 16	Conclusion	169
APPENDIX 1		173
APPENDIX 2		181
Bibliography		182

Acknowledgements

The author would like to record his sincerest appreciation of all who have so kindly assisted and shown interest in this study of the 'Clio' and in particular:

1. Mrs Cole-Edwards, Menai Bridge, and Miss Adams, Bangor, who supplied many original   photographs.
2. Mr Campbell McMurray, National Maritime Museum. Miss Christine Walker, Home Office, and the staff of the Gwynedd Archives, Caernarfon.
3. Dr. B. L. Davies who encouraged and gave guidance during my research.
5. My wife Ann, and two children, Dwynwen and Richard, who had to 'live' with the 'Clio' for over four years.
6. Dwynwen, the typesetter at Gwasg Carreg Gwalch for all her care and attention to detail.

Summary

This study of the functions of an industrial training ship in North Wales aims to prove that there was a dual purpose for establishing the ship. Primarily to take care of, and train the 'street-Arabs' who were milling about at the foot of the social ladder during the second half of the nineteenth century. Secondly, to provide a more efficient and regular supply of seamen for the Royal Navy and the Mercantile Marine.

The ship was financed by private subscriptions, and aided by Government Grants. Although the 'Clio' was advertised as being for the poor respectable boys of North Wales and the border counties, it will be seen that the majority of the boys on board came from London, Birmingham, Manchester, and other large industrial towns.

In tracing the history of the development of the Industrial Training Ship System, especially the 'Clio', I have tried to compare the standards of education; the curriculum; the methods of teaching and training, and the living conditions on board, with other ships and shore schools. I have tried to bring in how the various Education Acts related indirectly to the Industrial Training Ship system, and how the system itself fitted in with the national system of education and the reformatory schools.

From the letters of a few of the 'Clio' old boys during the First World War it will be seen that the ship had served its purpose in educating 'street-Arabs' and in training boys for the sea. However, the ravages of time, the changing attitudes in the field of education, especially the implementation of the 1918 Education Act, saw the decline and finally the end of the Industrial Training Ship System.

CHAPTER 1

Introduction

On Saturday afternoon, 29th July, 1876, a public meeting was held at the County Hall, Beaumaris, Anglesey, 'for the purpose of promoting the object of having the proposed industrial training ship for North Wales, Chester and the border counties, moored in the Menai Strait, and not, as originally intended, in the Dee, at Mostyn Deep, off Queen's Ferry.' The meeting should have been presided over by Sir Richard L. M. Williams-Bulkeley, Bart., Baron Hill, but due to a family bereavement, he was unable to be present. In the absence of Sir Richard, the Mayor of Beaumaris, Dr. R. Wynne-Jones presided, and in his opening remarks alluded to the dual purpose of establishing the ship. The primary object was 'that all gutter children – street Arabs, or wastrel boys – whatever term might be used – should be taken care of and trained. These children were now under Act of Parliament, liable to be taken before the Magistrates and sent to an industrial training school or ship, whether they wished it or not, unless they were under efficient parental control or had guardians to look after them. It would be important to take these children out of their neglected station in life and put them in the way of earning their own livelihood in a proper manner.' Secondly, the intention was to 'provide a more efficient supply of seamen for the Royal Navy and the Mercantile Marine.'

The years 1850 to 1870 saw considerable political activity, resulting in Gladstone's Reform Parliament of 1868-74. The violence and poverty of the time, and the sharpness of social distinctions had meant a countryside 'plagued by a moving population of thousands who begged, peddled and thieved their way from one country to another.' The fear of the upper and middle classes was that there would always be an 'improvident, irresponsible mass, many of them potentially or actively criminal, milling about at the foot of the social ladder.'

The English system of education at this time was in many ways behind those of Scotland, France and Prussia. So far as education was involved in politics, the issue turned on the alleged virtual control of elementary education by the Established Church and on the disabilities of Nonconformists. Despite this, the discussions on education were prompted by a growing desire on all sides to see more and better schools of all kinds. The dissatisfaction generally felt in the 1860s gave rise to three important commissions, the Newcastle Commission to deal with elementary schools, the Clarendon and Taunton Commissions to deal with Public and endowed schools.

The time of prejudice against popular education was past. Few people now believed that it was dangerous for the poor to be able to read and write: opinion was strongly setting the other way. The implementation of W. E. Forster's Elementary Education Act of 1870 was a milestone from which there was no turning back. The weight of evidence at last was great enough to overcome the denominational difficulty and to push through the compromise which preserved the Dual System and enabled public authorities to fill the gaps in elementary education.

For those who advocated the state taking a part in British education the decade before the passing of the 1870 Elementary Education Act provided them with powerful arguments. First: that English education was known to be backwards in comparison with that of many continental countries, and the wars of the period 1860-70 seemed to show that an educated nation could provide better soldiers than a less educated rival.

11

The north beat the south in the United States and Prussia defeated Austria in Europe. Second: the Representation of the People Act of 1867 which extended the franchise and gave household suffrage to boroughs, subject to some qualifications, threatened the country with an illiterate democracy. Third: it was becoming obvious that voluntary efforts to build schools, especially in towns, were not keeping pace with the rapid increase in child population. In introducing his Bill, W. E. Forster estimated that 'there were 1,000,000 children unprovided for between 6 and 10, and half a million between 10 and 12 years of age.'

The previous two decades had not only shown that Britain was lagging behind its continental rivals in education but there was also the fear of competition in commerce and industry from the United States and Germany. However, the golden Victorian boom of British capitalism which had come about with the massive development of the capital goods industries – railways, iron and steel, as against the textiles of the earlier phase – meant that Britain as an island depended a great deal on its ability to export its goods all over the world. To do this it needed shipping. There was, therefore, great concern about our naval resources. In the words of Morgan Lloyd, Q.C.,M.P., 'Our speciality being commerce and shipping, it was our special duty to do what we could to render the shipping of the highest possible class (because) of all the steam-tonnage in the world, two-thirds was owned by British shipowners and sailed under the British flag.' Unfortunately these ships were manned by men 'who were a disgrace to the name of sailor – men who committed murder and mutinied, and were insubordinate', and were in the main foreigners of dubious character.

The consequent concern about our naval and mercantile resources led to the Royal Commission of 1858, 'On Manning the Navy'. The recommendations of the Commissioners, published in 1859, provided a plan, which was never put into

12

operation, for safeguarding the future supply of recruits from the volunteer reserve. 'These proposals must have had an indirect but powerful influence upon the growth of the school ships in the latter half of the century.' The proposals were that school ships should be established in the main commercial ports, capable of accommodating from 120 to 200 boarders in each ship, of whom 100 should be supported by the state. The boys should be of respectable parentage, strong and healthy, and if there were any problems in the method of selection it was generally felt that 'the inspectors employed by the Committee of the Council for Education would readily assist in obtaining from the different schools throughout the United Kingdom the requisite number.' The boys were to be sent for approval, medically and otherwise, to the coastguard ship, or the naval surgeon would attend on board the school ship to admit them. Besides the 100 boarders, the school would be open to all children residing at the ports, who would attend as day pupils and consequently pay their weekly contributions. While in the school the boys would receive the requisite instruction for a career in the merchant service, plus some of the 'peculiar instruction requisite for the Navy, gunnery, etc.'

It was further proposed that the school ships, intended principally to train boys for the merchant service, would be administered by the Registrar-General of shipping, and through him the Board of Trade. It was contemplated that when the system had been well established and had been proved successful in practice, that it would be found desirable to unite the training ships for the Royal Navy with those of the volunteer force and to train boys for both services on board the same ships.

Not all were happy about these proposals, however, and the comment of one of the Commissioners, Admiral Martin, was that 'to take boys from reformatories and prisons would be to incur the expense of training a class of men the least likely to be amenable to discipline and the most likely to abandon their country when they were most needed.'

Following the passing of the 1870 Elementary Education Act there was a strong opinion that as the state had determined that all children should henceforth be taught, school ships afloat should, as regards educational grants and inspection, be placed on the same footing as schools ashore, so far as boys who were not convicted or were not consigned were concerned.

The purpose of establishing the industrial training ships was therefore twofold. It was generally felt that with the state's determination to provide elementary education for all, the ships would become part of the country's educational system. The 'improvident, irresponsible mass, many of them potentially or actively criminal, milling about at the foot of the social ladder' would for the lack of a better word, be 'conscripted' to fill the ships. The ships in their turn would provide a regular and more efficient supply of seamen for the Mercantile Marine and the Royal Navy.

A great deal depended, as it had done for the provision of elementary education, on the philanthropic and financially secure upper and middle classes, who it was hoped would contribute towards the running of these ships. For the better-off classes it was by now very evident that the education of the children of the poor was a matter of conscience. As Mr Forster had declared in introducing his Elementary Education Act to the House of Commons in February, 1870, the government's intention was 'to complete the present voluntary system, to fill up the gaps, sparing the public money where it can be done without, procuring as much as we can the assistance of the parents, and welcoming as much as we rightly can the co-operation and aid of those benevolent men who desire to assist their neighbours.'

The co-operation and aid of the benevolent men would be needed in establishing the industrial training ships because in an age of 'laissez-faire' the state was quite prepared to encourage individual philanthropy and enterprise, and as with the Elementary Education Act it was quite happy to endorse these schemes at no great risk to itself by allocating grants. The benevolent and financially secure would derive some form of practical advantages from their benevolence by seeing the training ships as the natural cure for pauperism and crime, in the words of Mrs Helen Bosanquet – 'To a very large extent we have in London succeeded in putting a stop to the wholesale manufacture of pauperism and crime which had been going on. Perhaps the most important step towards its suppression was the Industrial Schools Act of 1866.'

CHAPTER 2

The Establishment of Industrial Training Ships

The means of supplying the Royal Navy and the Mercantile Marine with a steady flow of recruits and the problem of curing pauperism and crime, especially juvenile crime, amongst the seething mass at the foot of the social ladder, had plagued the British Government for many years. Even as far back as 1691 when the British fleets were manned by volunteers, a plan was proposed to meet an emergency, 'whereby every boy whose parents received alms was to be indentured and bound at the age of fourteen to the King, and sent to Greenwich to be educated for the sea.' All merchant ships were to be obliged to take one apprentice to every six or ten men, depending on the trades in which they were engaged. A certain proportion of these boys were to be sent on board the ships of war, while others were to be distributed to trades connected with the sea. Tradesmen such as carpenters, caulkers and sailmakers were bound to employ a certain number of these boys.

During the last decade of the Seventeenth-Century and the early years of the Eighteenth Century Acts of Parliament were passed for the 'furnishing and supplying His Majesty's Royal Navy with a competent number of able mariners and seamen, which my be in readiness at all times for sea service.' The object of these measures was to establish the necessity of enforcing the old law of impressment, but they were not successful in raising the required number of men, partly because the Government of those days failed to provide for the due payment of the bounties and wages promised. Also, the extreme severity and harshness of the service did nothing to improve the situation. These harsh conditions were to last well into the Nineteenth Century. Conditions that meant 'the sailor of 1816 was still subject to the lash. He could still be flogged round the fleet, so many lashes inflicted at the gangway of each ship. For very serious offences, such as mutiny, he could be sentenced to death and hanged on board. Awaiting court-martial, he could be gagged, and bound hand and foot, in irons, for indefinite periods. Grim punishments such as Keelhauling and spreadeagling belonged to the very recent past. Lesser punishments were 'toeing the line', that is, standing on the same spot on the quarter-deck for hours on end, or banishment to the rigging for half a day.'

All through the Eighteenth Century, well-meant efforts were made by the Admiralty to try and solve the problem of manning its navy. In those days, and in fact until nearly a century later, it was the rule during peace time to keep only a few ships commissioned and a small number of seamen on the active list, with no reserve of any kind to fall back upon. At the outbreak of war the personnel of the service had to be greatly increased at the shortest possible notice; and to effect this, money bounties were first offered to entice seamen to volunteer, and later the press gang, by forcible means, collected those who held back. Thus the ships and their crews more or less completed, but eventually as the war proceeded, and the supply of seamen fell short, landsmen, or men who had never been to sea, had to be enlisted.

It was at the outbreak of the seven years' war with France, in the year 1756, when efforts to man our ships had not met with great success, that Mr Jonas Hanway, renowned as a great philanthropist in his day, and a man of some influence in the City of London, stirred up public feelings and induced a number of merchants and other gentlemen to start a society, under the name of the Marine Society, for encouraging landsmen to volunteer for service in the fleet – a complete uniform sea kit being offered to every volunteer accepted by the naval Regulating Captains. Mr Hanway's proposals were well received and generously supported financially, and so successfully carried out that 'between the years 1756 and 1812, no less than 39,360 landsmen were presented with these clothing bounties.'

The Marine Society's work in connection with the volunteers had but just commenced when application was made to the Society's Committee to extend its energies in another direction. By means of private subscription, raised by a Mr Fowler-Walker, a number of poor and distressed boys had for some months previously been collected and sent to serve in the King's ships by Mr John Fielding, a London magistrate. The funds for this work having all but run dry, the Marine Society was requested to carry it on, which the Committee willingly consented to do. Boys were collected from all parts of the country, fitted out with a seakit, similar in design to that presented to the landsmen volunteers, and were sent to the King's ships as servants. This branch of the Marine Society's work eventually became its main object, especially when the necessity for clothing landsmen ceased entirely with the deceleration of peace in 1815.

The work on behalf of the 'poor and distressed boys' was rigorously pursued along the same lines up to the year 1786, when it was considered desirable to give these boys some elementary training in their future profession before sending them to sea. On the proposal of Alderman Brook-Watson, a small merchant vessel, named the 'Beatty', was purchased, fitted up as a training ship, and stationed off Deptford, where every Marine Society boy received a short training before being drafted to sea. 'This ship is proudly claimed by the Society as being the pioneer of all training ships in this or any other country.' As Mr Whalley was later to mention in his speech at a

18

public meeting held at the Penrhyn Hall, Bangor, on Monday 4th September, 1876, to further the proposal of establishing the North Wales, Chester and Border Counties Industrial Training Ship; 'it was in 1758 that Mr Jonas Hanway hit upon the very scheme which they were now, it was hoped, in a fair way of maturing, and established the first voluntary training ship, and the Marine Society, which, existing to this day, has rescued from the streets and destitution and crime above 60,000.'

In 1854, with Palmerston as Home Secretary, 'An Act for the better care and Reformation of Youthful Offenders in Great Britain' was passed. It proposed that Reformatory Schools should be established by 'voluntary contributions' in various parts of Great Britain, and it was 'expedient that more extensive use should be made of these institutions.' The first step towards the realisation of this scheme was made by the Liverpool Juvenile Reformatory Association by the opening of the reformatory training ship 'Akbar' in 1856. The law provided for a committal of a period 'not less than two years and not exceeding five years' by the magistrates before whom a delinquent boy was brought.

The Royal Commission of 1858 'On Manning the Navy' which came about as the result of the breakdown in the manning of the Fleet at the outbreak of the Russian War in 1854, and the consequent concern about our naval and mercantile resources. The recommendations of the Commissioners published in 1859, provided a plan, which was never put into operation, but the proposals must have had an indirect influence on the growth of the school ships in the latter half of the century.

While the Commission was actually taking evidence negotiations were proceeding between the Admiralty and the Liverpool Mercantile Marine Association for the loan of a training ship. In July, 1858, an Admiralty order was issued for the loan of HMS 'Vestal', but this vessel was replaced by HMS

'Conway' in December, 1858. The 'Conway', as well as the 'Worcester' moored in the Thames, were, however, designed as colleges for the education of boys of good parentage and position in life and destined to serve as officers in the merchant service.

In 1856, an 'Act to amend the Mode of committing Criminal and Vagrant Children to Reformatory and Industrial Schools' was passed. This was quickly followed in 1857, by an 'Act to make better provision for the care and education of vagrant, destitute, and disorderly children, and for the extension of industrial schools.' In 1860, there was yet another Act to amend the previous one. This transferred the powers vested in the Committee of the Council on Education to the Secretary of State.

A further 'Act for amending and consolidating the Law relating to Industrial Schools' was passed in 1861. By this Act children liable to be sent to a certified industrial school were:

'1. Any child apparently under the age of fourteen years found begging or receiving alms, or being in any street or public place for the purpose of begging or receiving alms;

2. Any child apparently under the age of fourteen years that is found wandering, and not having any home or settled place of abode, or any visible means of subsistence, or frequents the company of reputed thieves;

3. Any child apparently under the age of twelve years who, having committed an offence punishable by imprisonment or some less punishment, ought nevertheless, in the opinion of the Justices, regard being had to his age, and to the circumstances of the case, to be sent to an Industrial School;

4. Any child under the age of fourteen years whose parent represents that he is unable to control him, and that he desires such child to be sent to an Industrial School, in pursuance of this Act, and who at the same time gives such undertaking or other security as may be approved by the Justices before whom he is brought, in pursuance of this Act, to pay all expenses incurred

for the maintenance of such child at school;

Provided that no child who, on being brought before the Justices, is proved to have been previously convicted of Felony, shall be deemed to be within the provisions of this Act.'

It was also stated that 'no child shall in pursuance of this Act be detained against his consent in any certified Industrial School after he has attained the age of fifteen years.' This Act was to 'remain in force until the first day of January, 1864.'

Two Acts were to follow in 1866; 'An Act to consolidate and amend the Acts relating to Industrial Schools in Great Britain', and 'An Act to consolidate and amend the Acts relating to Reformatory Schools in Great Britain.' It must not be assumed that either of these two Acts were designed expressly for establishing ships; there is no mention of such an intention in either Act. However, the distinction between industrial schools and reformatory schools is important. The difference is perhaps best demonstrated by the definitions given in the Children's Act, 1908. 'Reformatory School means a school for the industrial training of youthful offenders, in which youthful offenders are lodged, clothed, and fed, as well as taught', whereas, an 'industrial school means a school for the industrial training of children, in which children are lodged, clothed, and fed, as well as taught.'

The difference then was simple; a boy who had been convicted of a crime could not be received into an industrial school. This was important in establishing the ships, because the conditions of entry into the Royal Navy were that a 'boy *must* be of good character, able to read and write, and have the written consent of his parent or guardian to his entry. A lad who has been in a reformatory cannot be entered.'

During the twenty years, 1860-1880, the following industrial training ships were established:

'Havannah', off Cardiff, 1861;

'Wellesley', on the River Tyne, 1868;

21

'Southampton', off Hull, 1868;
'Cumberland', later 'Empress', on the Clyde, 1869;
'Mars', off Dundee, 1869;
'Formidable', off Bristol, 1869;
'Gibraltar', off Belfast, 1872;
'Mount Edgcumbe', off Plymouth, 1877;
'Shaftesbury', off Grays, Essex, 1877;
and the 'Clio', off Bangor, also in 1877.

These ships were the results of that voluntary philanthropic movement, which at the end of the Eighteenth Century and the beginning of the Nineteenth Century attacked the old prison system. The general hope of the benevolent men involved in establishing these training ships being that the training ship boy would develop 'from a rough, uncouth, undisciplined boy, into a smart, clean, well set-up youth, benefited both in mind and body by some months of good feeding and systematic mental and bodily training. All that a training ship can do for a boy is to turn him out, not a ready-made sailor, but a decent, orderly being prepared to quickly assimilate a sailor's duties, and with the groundwork of his future profession more or less laid.'

The ships were, therefore, to be the means of supplying the Royal Navy and the Mercantile Marine with a steady flow of recruits and at the same time a way of solving the problem of pauperism and juvenile crime amongst the seething mass at the foot of the social ladder.

CHAPTER 3

Establishing the Industrial
Training Ship 'Clio'

The 'Chester Chronicle' of the 5th February, 1876, proudly proclaimed that 'the Dee Training Ship project is now fairly before the public, who are invited to aid by their donations and annual subscriptions in the successful establishment of such an invaluable institution, accessible to the populous districts of North Wales and Cheshire as it will undoubtedly prove to be.' His Grace, the Duke of Westminster who headed the subscription list with a donation of £300, had accepted the office of President. The Lord-Lieutenant of Denbighshire and the Lord-Lieutenant of Flintshire had both accepted the office of vice-president. A representative general committee, along with a provisional executive committee, had been set up, 'after careful deliberation, and acting under official advice' they selected Mostyn Deep as the site for the ship. The article concluded by stating that requests for any information on the subject, or donations, should be sent to the Hon. Secretary, Capt. Moger, R.N., Bryn Alyn, Gresford.

Capt. Moger had been involved in the inaugural meeting, held at Wrexham in January, 1875. This meeting had came about following a suggestion by a Canon Kingsley that it would be of interest to establish a training ship on the Dee. The idea was taken up by a group of influential gentlemen who thought that it would 'be an excellent thing to have such a ship for poor destitute, or neglected boys belonging to the Principality and the adjoining counties on the Dee.'

There followed another public meeting, again held at Wrexham, in February, 1875, where it was unanimously resolved to establish an industrial training ship for North Wales, Cheshire and the border counties. However, 'at the suggestion of the Board of Trade it was deemed expedient to wait the result of the Merchant Shipping Act of 1875, which had an important bearing on this subject.' The Bill was not carried successfully through parliament and consequently all it had done was to delay the movement.

Gradually the movement gathered momentum and was getting more and more publicity in the local press. The newly formed committee would have been a credit to any modern advertising agency in their attempts to publicise their movement. The local newspapers carried such patriotic statements as 'Thanks to Mr Plimsoll, we are to have better ships, let us also have better sailors.' – 'Over and over again it has been shown that both the navy and the mercantile marine are indebted in a great measure to training ships for their best men, and if England is to retain its supremacy as the first naval force in the world, and the first commercial nation, it is most essential that our sailors should be carefully trained to their work.'

There were those, however, who had grave doubts about the purpose of establishing the ship, and the committee felt it expedient to 'correct an error in which many have fallen, it being the belief that the establishment of a ship in the Dee would withdraw boys from remunerative labour in collieries, manufactories and other industries. But this is not so, as it is for homeless, destitute, and poor boys, that the institution is designed.'

By march, 1876, a suitable site had been selected for the ship, 'at the south-east end of Mostyn Deep, where she will be within half a mile of the shore at high tide, the holding ground is excellent and the shelter good.' The money subscribed for the purpose of establishing the ship was far short of the required amount and an appeal was to be made by the committee to the mercantile community and the Welshmen of Liverpool to help out. The committee had by now been offered by the Admiralty 'the choice of two disused line-of-battle ships, namely, the 'Albion', 3,117 tons, and 'St George', 2,864 tons, now lying at Davenport.'

Of the two ships, Capt. Moger had selected the 'St George' as being the most suitable for their purpose. It was estimated that £5,000 would be required to fit her up, and since donations had only reached £1,900, some £3,000 was still needed. About £800 would be required annually to run the ship. However, 'the Admiralty had promised to give £25 for every boy that joined the Navy after two years training, and £3 for every boy that joined the Naval Reserve, but these boys must come up to a certain standard.'

Following the meeting held at Beaumaris, which had originally been instigated to acquire funds and donations from the landed gentry and monied people of Anglesey and Caernarfonshire, it was generally felt that the Menai Strait was a more suitable place to moor the ship than Mostyn Deep. As the *North Wales Chronicle* reported, 'A large number of the county gentry took an interest in the movement, and many had promised contributions conditionally on the vessel being moored in the Straits.'

There followed another meeting at the Town Hall, Chester, on the following Saturday, presided over by the Duke of Westminster. Dr. Eyton Jones, the Mayor of Wrexham, moved 'that owing to the large amount of subscriptions and interest from that part, it was desirable that the ship be moored in the Menai Strait.' The motion was seconded by Capt. Verney and was carried without dissent. The Duke of Westminster was also inclined to think 'though that removed the ship from Cheshire further than was intended, that it would be a more desirable site than Mostyn Deep.'

The committee now needed to establish itself in the area of the Menai Strait, and on Monday, 4th September, 1876, arranged two 'important and influential public meetings' at the Penrhyn Hall, Bangor. The afternoon meeting was presided over by Lord Penrhyn, the Lord Lieutenant of Caernarfonshire, and he was supported on the platform by the Bishop of Bangor, Mr Watkin Williams, QC., MP, Mr Morgan Lloyd, QC, MP, Mr G. H. Whalley, MP, the Ven. Archdeacon Wynne Jones, Alderman Hugh Humphreys (Mayor of Caernarfon), Dr. Wynne Jones (Mayor of Beaumaris), Dr. Brisco Owen (Ex-Mayor of Beaumaris), Mr F. W. Lloyd Edwards (Nanhoron), and Capt. Moger. The hall was well filled, and the *North Wales Chronicle* report of the following Saturday gives an impressive list of local dignitaries and influential people who were present.

Lord Penrhyn, in opening the proceedings, felt that it was not necessary for him to enter at any great length into an explanation of the objects of the proposed establishment of a training ship in the Menai Strait. This matter had been fairly well covered in the local press during the past year. However, he wanted to make quite sure that his audience 'were well aware of the advantages to be derived from these institutions when well managed, in rescuing from lives of ignorance and vice hundreds who would otherwise have been lost not only to usefulness in the country, but would have lived to swell the calendars of crime, and filled our prisons, and disgraced our records.' His lordship then alluded to the very striking incident which happened at the beginning of the year, – the burning of the training ship 'Goliath' in the Thames, 'when examples were given by those children which showed that under most trying circumstances they could exhibit habits of subordination, obedience to orders, regularity, and courage.'

Institutions, like the proposed training ship, though assisted by the Government, were mainly dependent upon contributions by private individuals, and Lord Penrhyn reminded his audience that the object of the meeting was to know how far the public in the neighbourhood were ready to assist in establishing a training ship in the Straits', and with what degree of cordiality they would answer the appeal made to them.' His lordship explained that he had not taken a great deal of interest in the movement until he had heard, in London, that it was proposed to transfer the site for the ship from the Dee to the Menai Strait. Since the Menai Strait were very narrow, and 'there were gentlemen having residential property on both sides', it would have been wrong for him to promote the transfer without knowing the opinion of these gentlemen, and giving them an opportunity of objecting if they wished to do so. There had been many meetings and opportunities for them to object to the scheme, and since no one had complained, he had decided to support the movement. The statement was greeted with raptuous applause.

The Bishop of Bangor was asked to propose the first resolution. This he did rather reluctantly, because of the 'very small amount of knowledge he was able to bring to the subject', and he believed the motion should have been put forward by someone confined to naval affairs. The motion was 'That owing to the large amount of subscriptions already promised, and the great interest felt in the matter in North Wales, it was desirable the training ship be moored in the Menai Strait, between Beaumaris and the Bridges.'

'The experienced secretary of the present movement, Capt. Moger', had, however, made sure that the Bishop would have some information and knowledge to draw upon, and had supplied him that very morning with a 'memorandum' from Mr Thomas Gray, of the Board of Trade. There were one or two sentences in Mr Gray's paper which struck the Bishop as being rather forcible, and he believed it was his duty to read them to the meeting. It was rather a lengthy paragraph, but it is worth quoting in full because of its suggestion that 'poor respectable parents' would object to the opportunities and education offered to the 'street-Arabs', and from which their children would have been barred.

The Bishop read the following extracts from Mr Gray's 'memorandum' – 'I would, however, recommend you (and this is a indeed very important point, and it will assure more importance in the future) also to look beyond the Industrial School classes for your boys, and with this view so frame the rules as to allow for admission of boys who are neither homeless nor destitute. There is no objection to the two classes mixing together on board the same ship, they do so on many ships at present, and I assure you and I speak from personal knowledge and inspection of every ship, that the homeless soon forget their homelessness and their bad associates and bad example, and rapidly become bright, lively and healthy lads, amenable to discipline, ready, clever and obedient, and above all cleanly in their speech and habits. Therefore, do not let any false sentimentality interfere with your endeavours to provide for two classes of boys in one ship, where they are well cared for and looked after. Another special reason why you should provide for the reception of boys who have been kept out of the gutter, is that these boys ought not to be handicapped in the race with gutter boys. *The so-called 'respectable' poor boy ought to have at least as fair a chance of participating in the great benefits afforded by training ships and in the battle of life as the so-called 'street-Arabs', whereas at present, the latter has an immense advantage over the former. The latter is partly supported by the Treasury, the former gets help from nobody.'*

The Bishop continued by saying that although poor respectable parents might object to their children being banned from a good education and being launched under favourable circumstances into life, there were others who would object to their children 'associating with those who had been brought up in circumstances not so happy as themselves, and they might fear that their morals would be corrupted.' He felt it was their duty at least to give the experiment of combining the two 'classes' a fair trial.

The resolution to establish the ship in the Straits was seconded by the Mayor of Beaumaris. He was happy to hear that the locality of the ship was not objectionable to the landed gentry of the district, as Sir Richard Bulkeley, for one, had suggested that he had not the least objection to the proposed site of mooring the ship.

Lord Penrhyn then read a letter, which had been addressed to Capt. Moger, from Admiral Lord Clarence Paget with advice on the best position to moor the ship in the Straits. On the whole, he thought the most eligible position for the ship would be off Garth Ferry, for there was room there for her to swing. However, it was essential that they should have on shore, near the ship, a small space of about half an acre where they could repair the boats. If there was any objections to this place, then he would suggest that a good and possibly more roomy berth might be found for her between Llanidan and Llanfair, abreast of Griffith's Crossing, where she would be close to Portinorwic, with a railway station near her, and a good flat beach which would be very handy. Unfortunately, here she would not be so accessible to visitors, and of the two sites, he preferred the one off Garth Ferry.

Captain Moger endorsed Lord Clarence's suggestion by reading a letter from the hydrographer to the Admiralty who agreed that an anchorage in 'Bangor Pool appeared to be as good a place as any in the Menai Strait for the 'St George' to be moored.'

This apparently did not please the Mayor of Caernarfon, who stepped forward and reminded Lord Penrhyn that the meeting at Chester had only decided to substitute the Straits in lieu of Mostyn Deep. The exact point of the site had not been decided there and he wished to know whether the present meeting had to decide that point. Possibly with a mooring place nearer to Caernarfon in mind, he pointed out that there were other sites equally as good as those suggested.

Lord Penrhyn replied that he did not suppose it was intended that the present meeting should decide any point, but merely express an opinion with regard to the present proposed site. It was open for any meeting, at Caernarfon or elsewhere, to suggest a different site, then the matter could be decided by a joint committee representing the various counties.

The Bishop of Bangor's resolution was then put to the meeting and was carried unanimously.

Mr Watkin Williams, QC, MP, moved the next resolution, 'That this meeting pledges itself, individually and collectively, to assist in carrying out the project with as little delay as possible.' He then moved into a rather controversial speech by first attacking the Eisteddfod. He wished his countrymen would show 'as much enthusiasm and working ardour on behalf of an institution of this kind, as they showed in the maintenance of the Eisteddfod. He had nothing to say against eisteddfodau, but he did think sometimes considering the enormous number of persons that collected on those occasions and the money spent, that the bards and Druids representing a long past era – many centuries ago – were more interested in that epoch than in 1876.' It was a statement that was greeted with laughter and applause.

The Member of Parliament for Denbigh District then jibbed at the fervent Welshmen who had fought so hard to establish the University at Aberystwyth by suggesting that the establishing of the training ship 'was of great practical importance, and which he ranked in the same category as the college at Aberystwyth.'

His next target was Lord Penrhyn himself. Mr Williams confessed that he was a little surprised when Lord Penrhyn had referred to a possible doubt that owners of land and houses on the banks of the Straits would have had about the value of having the training ship in their locality. He reminded Lord Penrhyn that he himself was old enough to remember magnets opposing with all their power the establishment of a railway to a port that would give communication with Ireland. When it had been proposed that a railway should go through Merioneth, all the landed gentry concerned thought that everything that was bad was to follow and they had done their utmost to stop that railway. However, by now these gentlemen were doing their utmost to get railways constructed through their properties.

Rather condescendingly, Mr Williams was inclined to agree with Lord Penrhyn, and the Bishop of Bangor, that these training ships should not only accept boys not convicted of crime, but tainted with it, but that they should also be open to the children of respectable parents. Were not the towns, villages, and country districts teeming with young lads, full of life, energy, and ability, who with their qualities misdirected were the most dangerous, and were liable to run into crime? Not missing an opportunity, the Member for Denbigh District confessed that he had sympathy for poachers, because these lads were determined, spirited and independent, 'but perhaps they made the squire and parson a little uncomfortable?' This class of men had made England what it was, men who had made our Nelsons and Wellingtons', men who galled at the position they were placed in, and were not quiet, timid citizens.' Mr Williams felt that if it had been his destiny to be pinned down without any career before him, he should probably have been a poacher himself.

Finally he came to the point and stated that the demand for seamen at the present time was four or five times more than it was some years ago. 'The truth was that demand was so enormous that the supply, even if it were superior to that of twenty or thirty years ago, is not equal to demand.' Concluding, he hoped that before many months went over their heads they would be able to say 'that the Welsh people could not only promote singing, prose and poetry, and the cultivation of fine arts and such like, but they could put their shoulders to matters of practical moment, and show Englishmen they could do solid work which would be sure to be of great usefulness and value to the country.'

It was rather a subdued Mr F. W. Lloyd Edwards who seconded the resolution. Lord Penrhyn was not so subdued and he wished to explain that when he said he had at first been disinclined to take an active part in the movement and in the selection of a site in the Menai Strait, he had done so because he desired to ascertain what the feelings of the other landed proprietors were before he took an active part. He did not think he was in any way wrong in doing that, and should it happen again he would do the same thing.

Mr Morgan Lloyd, QC, MP, stood up to address the meeting and second the resolution. He felt it was unnecessary for him to say much to add to what had already been said. However, amongst the few observations he wished to make were that 'Our speciality being commerce and shipping, it was our special duty to do what we could to render the shipping of the highest possible class, and also to train for the maritime service seamen superior to any other seamen on the face of the globe.' He also believed that 'They, in Wales, in modern times, never liked to be behind the people of England. Whether they were behind them or not he would not stop to inquire; but they wished to be abreast of them; and among other things they wished to be abreast of the English in education. Hence the movement to establish a college at Aberystwyth.' This was his opportunity to get back at his fellow Member of Parliament. Since mention of the Eisteddfod had been made, 'He believed it was a grand institution.' A statement greeted with loud applause by the audience. Was he beginning to turn the gathering, or had the two Members of Parliament, who were also Queen's Counsels, worked it that they would, in a modern idiom, 'milk the audience'? He continued by claiming that the Eisteddfod had done great things for this country, and he believed that the very spirit which had been manifested in maintaining the Eisteddfod would in due course be equally manifested by the Welsh people in maintaining other institutions. The Eisteddfod was an old institution; the Welsh liked old things as well as new, and they liked to improve old things. They had taken up the Eisteddfod and had improved it, and it was now in a much better position than it was ten years ago. He reminded the meeting that the Welsh people had taken up the movement of establishing a college at Aberystwyth with a vigour which had not been exceeded in England, Scotland or Ireland. He would not have mentioned either the Eisteddfod or the College, except that they had been mentioned by a previous speaker, and he thought it was only fair to refer to them in order 'to show that the Welsh people will take up warmly anything they are satisfied is for the benefit of the country.'

Concluding his address Mr Morgan Lloyd stated that since Wales did not have the criminal population to send aboard the ship, he saw it as an opportunity 'for poor lads who had not the means of having the simplest education, but who yearned for advancement in life.' He believed the Straits to be the best place to moor the ship, and he was particularly in favour of having the ship as near the Isle of Anglesey as he possible could have her.

The second resolution having been carried unanimously it was Capt. Moger's turn to address the meeting and state their present financial position. Promises of donations up to £2,400 had been given towards fitting up the ship; double this amount would be required. Over £400 had been promised towards defraying annual expenses, but even with the Admiralty Grants they were still short of their target.

A vote of thanks to the Chairman was proposed by Mr Whalley, MP, and seconded by Archdeacon Wynne Jones.

Lord Penrhyn in replying to the vote of thanks wished to thank all those who had addressed the meeting, but obviously still smarting from the attack by Mr Watkin Williams, he had to disagree with one honourable gentleman who believed 'that no man could be a Wellington or a Nelson unless he had been a poacher.' The proceedings terminated with an appeal for funds towards establishing the training ship.

The evening meeting was held at eight o'clock, and the Penrhyn Hall was again densely crowded. The chair was taken by Mr W. Bulkeley Hughes, MP, and he was supported on the platform by the Dean of Bangor, Capt. G. W. Bulkeley Hughes, Mr Whalley, MP, and Capt. Moger.

The chairman was happy to learn that there had been such a successful and well attended meeting in the same hall that afternoon. He was pleased to learn that the ship was to be stationed in the Straits, as he failed to see why the Dee and Mersey should monopolise these training ships. He was an advocate 'for education of every description without regard to sect or conditions.' Perhaps some of the boys in the audience to-night would eventually distinguish themselves, not only in the navy or army, but likewise in the college at a future period.

Capt. Moger was asked to explain the objects of establishing a training ship in the locality. In the course of his remarks he said that having visited Mostyn Deep and seen the desolation thereof, he had come to the decision that the Menai Strait were a much better place for mooring the 'St George', and those who had subscribed with the intention of having the ship placed in the Dee had concurred that she should rather be stationed in the Straits.

As we have seen, Capt. Moger had been involved from the outset in establishing this training ship. From the first meeting in Wrexham in January, 1875; he was Honorary Secretary to the movement; he had decided on the 'St George' as being the most suitable ship; he had made sure that all the speakers for the

34

cause had the relevant information, and he had just claimed that having seen the desolation on Mostyn Deep, he had decided on the Menai Strait as being a more suitable mooring point. He now believed, 'but one was never quite sure of anything mundane – that he should have command of the 'St George' when she came here.' However, he wanted to assure the meeting that 'he had not wanted, in this movement, to promote self-interests. His first object was not to serve himself, but to do something for the poor, neglected boys.' Having entered the navy at the time of the Crimean War, he had been twenty years at sea, and had been in command of a training ship at Plymouth where he had already trained upwards of 2,000 boys for the navy. Capt. Moger completed his speech by giving a statement of the movement's financial situation.

Mr Whalley, MP, then gave a brief history of the training ship movement up until that time. He drew the meeting's attention to the fact that he had given notice at the Eisteddfod, recently held at Wrexham, that he would give a prize of £25 for an essay on Training Ships, which would be competed for at the Caernarfon Eisteddfod the following year. In conclusion he moved a similar resolution to the one adapted in the afternoon meeting.

The Dean of Bangor seconded the motion 'in an eloquent Welsh speech'. He alluded to the afternoon meeting as being one of the most interesting that had been held for a long time. Mr Watkin Williams, he thought, had made an excellent speech that afternoon, and had spoken about boys of spirit, who were not fitted to become scholars, professional men, or tradesmen, but who disliked a quite life. They had energy, and that energy was often misdirected, because they had no better opportunities. Many a 'wild' lad got into mischief and became fond of poaching. These lads, though not possessed of scholastic talents, yet possessed courage, determination and 'pluck', and out of this material heroes were made. The Dean was sure that many poor families would be relieved to hear that subscribers of £25 could nominate a boy to be sent on board to be trained. 'There was nothing more necessary for a boy than to teach him to work and to be orderly, and respect and obey his superiors or leaders.' The Dean then referred to the burning of the training ships 'Warspite' and 'Goliath', on which occasion the lads on board, instead of fleeing in fright stood at their posts bravely, and endeavoured to extinguish the flames.' The little fellows had been taught order, and to obey, also to see the benefit of discipline.' He concluded by hoping that the general public would support the movement, and give Capt. Moger the support he deserved. The motion was then carried with much applause.

Capt. Bulkeley Hughes moved the second resolution, which was also identical with that of the afternoon meeting. The resolution was seconded, in Welsh, by Mr Lewis of Gantherwen. Mr John Roberts, assistant overseer, supported in a stirring Welsh speech, and also moved, 'That this meeting is of opinion that it is desirable to form a committee of working men, for the purpose of collecting subscriptions towards the training ship to be stationed in the Menai Strait.'

Mr John Price, Vice-Principal of the Bangor Normal College, and Chairman of the Bangor School Board, seconded Mr Roberts's proposition, and the resolution was carried with enthusiasm.

A vote of thanks to the Chairman was moved by Mr Whalley, and Mr Bulkeley Hughes in acknowledging it intimated his intention to place five poor lads on board the ship. The declaration was greeted with loud cheers and the meeting came to a close at ten o'clock.

Plans went ahead rapidly to collect as much money as possible. 'Training Ship Concerts' were held in Bangor and Beaumaris. These caused some friction since some of the artistes had given to understand that they would give their service gratuitously, instead they were claiming rather heavy 'expenses'. A Mrs Taylor Harrison had brought out 'an interesting little pamphlet' – 'The Training Ship Story' – the proceeds from the sale of which were to be devoted to the project.

There followed many meetings, and by the end of 1876, the committee had decided that their original idea of fitting out such a large ship as the 'St George' was out of their reach financially. The ship 'Clio' had now been obtained from the Admiralty, and was undergoing alterations. It was expected that the 'Clio', with accommodation for 150 boys, would be at her moorings by February, 1877.

The Executive Committee of the 'Clio' Training Ship Society met at the Town Hall, Chester, on Saturday, 27th January, 1877, and the following resolution was unanimously adopted: 'Understanding that it would be in accordance with the views of the Admiralty that the engines and boilers be removed from the 'Clio', as stated in the letter of Capt. Cordington to His Grace the Duke of Westminster, dated January 25th, 1877 – it was resolved that the suggestion of the Board of Admiralty in this respect be acceded to, viz: That the work required to be done before the 'Clio' can be towed to Bangor, estimated at about £150, be put in hand at once by the Admiralty at the expense of the Society; that the engines and boilers be removed in contemplation of the ship being sufficiently large to accommodate the people to be put in her permanently, subject to any claims that may in that respect be submitted to and approved by their lordships; that the 'Clio' should be towed to Bangor at the convenience of the Admiralty, and that all proper arrangements will be made by the Committee for mooring at Bangor, it being understood that the moorings be provided by the Admiralty, ride letter dated 7th December, 1876.' The meeting was also informed that the duties of Honorary Secretary would now be undertaken by Mr H. T. Brown, Solicitor, of Chester.

The committee's hopes of having the 'Clio' at her moorings by February, 1877 were dashed due to the Admiralty being unable to get anyone to undertake the work. By the beginning of March, however, a contract had been entered into with a firm on the Thames, 'for the speedy fitting-out of the 'Clio',' and the ship's engines and boilers were to be removed at Chatham. It was now confidently expected that the vessel would be in the Menai Strait by the end of May at the latest

This was not to be, and she was now expected at the end of July, with Capt. Moger on board. The committee was also anxious about the sub-committees which were appointed to canvass the City of Bangor, who had, they believed, been very lax, and complaints had been made that very little work or progress had been accomplished. They suggested that the gentlemen who had volunteered to do the work should not continue with it, but to give way to others who would be glad to take their places.

By the beginning of July a Government hulk was lying in the Straits awaiting the arrival of the moorings for the 'Clio', which were to be laid down in Bangor Pool, between Garth Ferryhouse and Glyn y Garth, on the Anglesey side of the Straits. The formal opening was fixed for Monday, 20th August, 1877. Mr Morgan, the Lessee of the Garth Ferries, had kindly agreed to boats belonging to the 'Clio' the privilege of using his landing stages free of toll.

On Saturday, 7th August, 1877, the 'Clio' finally arrived in the Menai Strait, 'in charge of Capt. Moger, R.N., with whom the proposal for such a ship originated, and had been carried out, and who had been appointed Captain-Superintendent.' The ship had been towed from Sheerness by the Admiralty's tug 'Sampson'; a voyage not without incident. The 'Clio' after leaving Sheerness, met with very rough weather, and when off Land's End, on the Wednesday night, was caught in a gale and sustained some damage. The 'Valorous' gunboat, in whose charge she left Sheerness, lost contact with the 'Clio' at the outbreak of the storm. Her arrival in Bangor Pool created a great deal of interest, and the Bangor boatmen 'drove an active trade in rowing visitors to the vessel.'

Even though it was Eisteddfod week in Caernarfon, excitement about the opening of the 'Clio' was mounting in Bangor to the extent that it was suggested that the 'tradesmen of Bangor should close their establishments for at least part of that day.' At the Eisteddfod Sir Llewelyn Turner read the adjudication of himself, Gwyneddon, and Mr Thomas Farning Evans, on the essays in Welsh and English on 'The Industrial Training Ship for North Wales and the Border Counties, moored in the Menai Strait; its physical, social and moral advantages.' The first prize of £10.10s. was awarded to 'Gwladgarwr', the nom-de-plume of Mr Owen Parry, Daily Press Office, Bristol.

Monday, 20th August dawned, and in Bangor, and on the Menai Strait, the rain came down in torrents the whole morning, but fortunately by the afternoon it had eased off. By about half past three there were several hundred people on board the 'Clio', a number of boats having been employed for some hours in conveying them there. The ship was decorated with 'a profuse display of bunting', and the guests were greeted on board by the music of the 'Indefatigable' training ship, Liverpool.

His Grace the Duke of Westminster having asked the Bishop of Bangor to offer up a prayer, proceeded to address those assembled on board. He gave them a brief history of the movement; how the ship came to be moored in the Straits; its purpose there; and referring to the derivation of the ship's name, added that the muse would not be out of place in the noble country surrounding it. Lord Penrhyn thanked the Duke on behalf of those present, and asked for three hearty cheers for the Duke and Duchess. On the motion of Mr S. Baker, a similar compliment was paid Lord and Lady Penrhyn.

The official opening ceremony being over the visitors proceeded to view the ship and to patronise a bazaar held 'between-decks' under the superintendence of Mrs Moger. All that was needed now was the issue of an Home Office Certificate and the 'Clio' would be ready to receive the boys.

The Industrial School Ship 'Clio' was certified to receive 200 boys on the 29th August, 1877. Before the boys were to arrive, there were unfortunately some complaints about the establishment of the ship and Mr Whalley was 'becoming weary of the correspondence respecting the Training Ship Clio', especially one letter writer who, unless he disclosed his name to Mr Whalley he would notice 'no more of his remarkable communications!' The only objection Mr Whalley knew of so far, had been from a 'Roman Catholic gentleman of influence in the district', who had stated that he would do his utmost to oppose the establishing of anything Mr Whalley was involved with. The correspondent had referred 'to some Protestant tower' of which he knew nothing, and he did not think it right for him to 'form or act upon conjectures as to his identity.'

On Monday, 8th October, 1877, the Liverpool School Board resolved 'That the Board do make with the Managers of the Training Ship 'Clio' in the Menai Strait, arrangements for the reception of boys committed under the 14th and 15th Section of the Industrial Schools Act by a Liverpool Magistrate with the concurrence of this Board – similar to those already made with the Managers of the Liverpool Industrial Schools, except that the amount of the Board's contribution towards the maintenance of each child so committed be 1s. 6d. instead of 1s. per week.'

The idea that the 'Clio' was being established primarily for the benefit of 'local' boys was rapidly beginning to disintegrate. A week before the Liverpool School Board meeting, a meeting of the Bangor School Board had been held. Unfortunately, only the Chairman, Mr Price, and Mr J. Hughes were present, and therefore not enough to constitute a quorum. The meeting was attended by Mr F. O. Ruspine, Clerk to the Manchester School Board, and since no business of an official character could be transacted what ensued was of an unofficial nature. Mr Ruspine explained to the two gentlemen present that he had come to ask the Bangor School Board for a favour, which they in Manchester might at some future time be able to reciprocate. He went on to state that the Manchester School Board had under their charge from time to time a great number of boys sent to school under the Industrial Schools Act, and that they drafted them in batches to training ships. They had already fifty aboard the 'Wellesley', and they proposed to place another fifty on the 'Clio'. They naturally felt a great responsibility, Mr Ruspine continued, and thought that an inspection of and a report on the condition of the unfortunate lads should be made, possibly every six months. This was an expense he would ask the Bangor School Board to save them at Manchester. He wished to know whether they would help them by making the inspection instead of them, and all he could offer in return was for the Manchester School Board to do something similar for them. After some discussion Mr Price, the Chairman, could see no objections to Mr Thomas, the Clerk, and himself visiting the 'Clio' once a year to report upon the condition of the Manchester boys.

October, 1877, saw Sir Llewelyn Turner giving a lecture on board HMS 'Eagle', moored in the Mersey, on the 'Life of Nelson'; the proceeds from the sale of tickets were donated to the 'Clio' fund. The same month Dr. R. E. Owen of Beaumaris was appointed honorary surgeon to the 'Clio', and by the beginning of December there were seven boys on board the vessel.

By Christmas there were twenty-one boys on board the 'Clio', and following an appeal for gifts and donations in the *North Wales Chronicle*, Capt. and Mrs Moger had arranged to give the boys a special tea on New Year's Eve, and to have a

Christmas tree 'with some little article on it for each boy'. Another six boys had now arrived on the ship, bringing the total to twenty-seven. This number was expected to double within the first fortnight of 1878, to bring the total number of boys on board the 'Clio' to fifty-four.

CHAPTER 4

Conditions under which boys could be sent to the Industrial Training Ship 'Clio'

A Certified Industrial School, or Ship, such as the 'Clio', was a school for the industrial training of children, in which those children were lodged, clothed, and fed, as well as taught. The fact that the 'Clio' was a 'certified' school meant that it was open to inspection, at least once a year, by the Chief Inspector of Reformatory and Industrial Schools, or by an inspector or assistant inspector. Perhaps one should also point out here that schools established under the Works School System and which were sometimes known as 'industrial schools' were not 'industrial training schools', but schools where 'employers of labour provided excellent elementary schools for their populations gathered within the centres of heavy industries and coalmining.'

The conditions under which a boy could be sent to the 'Clio', or any other Industrial Training School, or Ship, had been laid down in the Industrial Schools Act of 1866. This Act allowed any person to bring before two Justices or a Magistrate any child under fourteen years of age that came within any of the following descriptions: A child found begging or receiving alms (whether actually under the pretext of selling or offering for sale anything), or being in the street or public place for the purpose of begging or receiving alms. A child that was found wandering, homeless, or without a settled place of abode, or proper Guardianship, or had no visible means of subsistence. Any child that was found destitute, either being an orphan or having a

43

surviving parent who was undergoing penal servitude or imprisonment, or any child that frequented the company of reputed thieves. The Justices or Magistrate before whom the child was brought under any of the above descriptions, if satisfied, after making enquiries, about the child's condition, could then order him to be sent to a Certified Industrial School.

If a child 'apparently' under the age of twelve years was brought to Court and was charged with an offence that was punishable by imprisonment or a lesser punishment, due regard being taken of his age and the circumstances of the case, he also could be sent to an Industrial Training School. However, this was on condition that he had not been in England convicted of felony, or in Scotland of theft.

A child that a parent, step-parent or Guardian had brought before a Court as being beyond their control could be sent to an Industrial Training School. The court could also send to an Industrial Training School, at the request of the Guardians of the Poor of a Union, Parish Board of Guardians, Board of Management of a District Pauper School, or the Parochial Board of a Parish, any child, if under 14 years of age and was maintained in a Workhouse or Pauper School of a union or Parish, or in a District Pauper School, or in the Poorhouse of a Parish, that had wilfully broken any of their rules, or if his parents had been imprisoned for a crime.

Under the Prevention of Crimes Act, 1871, the children, if under 14 years of age, of any woman convicted of a crime, and with a previous conviction proved against her, and who were deemed to be under her control and care at the time of the second crime, and who had no visible means of support, or were without proper guardianship, then they also could be sent to an Industrial Training School by order of a Court of Law.

Lord Sandon's Education Act of 1876, besides giving some relief to the managers of Voluntary Schools by raising the Government grant, ordering districts where School Boards had not been established to elect School Attendance Committees with the same compulsory powers over attendance as the School Boards, also put the onus on the parent for seeing that his child received adequate instruction in the three Rs. The Act stated that the parent of any child above the age of five was prohibited from allowing that child to be taken into full-time employment, or 'without reasonable excuse' neglected to provide efficient elementary instruction for that child, were then liable to certain penalties. The same penalties would also apply to any child found habitually wandering or not under proper control, or found in the company of 'rogues, vagabonds, disorderly persons or reputed criminals.' It became the duty of the local authority, after fair warning to the parent of any such children, to bring them before a court of summary jurisdiction who could compell those children to attend a school, unless there was a reasonable excuse for not sending them.

A court order of this kind was to be known as an 'attendance order'. The 'reasonable excuses' being that there was not a public elementary school within two miles of the child's home, measured along the nearest road, or that the child had been absent due to sickness or any other unavoidable cause.

If the 'attendance order' was not compiled with, or unless there was a 'reasonable excuse', the local authority could again complain to the court of summary jurisdiction. The penalty for not complying to the 'attendance order' was either a 'fine' of 5s. or an order to send the child to a Certified Day Industrial School. For a second offence of this nature, the 'order' was to send the child to a Day Industrial School, or if there was not a day school suitable for the child, then to an Industrial School.

On the other hand, if the local authority were informed by 'any person' of a child under their jurisdiction who was stated by that person to be liable to be compelled to attend school under the 1876 Education Act, or under the 1866 Industrial Schools Act, then the local authority were bound to take proceedings in court. This, however, did not relieve the local authority from the responsibility of performing their duty as stated in the 1876 Education Act.

Section 50 of the same Act, also stated that nothing in that Act should prejudice the effect of or deregate from any provision relating to the committal of children to Industrial Schools or the employment of children contained in any previous Act of Parliament which may have been more stringent in its provisions.

A payment of 7s. 6d. per week was required by the 'Clio's' Committee for every boy received on board the ship under any of the above mentioned Sections, but the Treasury would contribute 6s. of this if the boys were received under Sections 14 and 15 of the Industrial Schools Act, 1866, or 3s. in the case of boys received under Section 16 of the same Act and Sections 11 and 12 of the 1876 Education Act. However, no boy would be received on board under the age of 11, or above the age of 15, except by special resolution of the ship's Executive Committee.

The 'Clio' would accept on board boys, aged between 11 and 15, who had been nominated by any person who was interested in them, and was willing to contribute £20 per year for each boy, taking into consideration that the contribution could be guaranteed to the satisfaction of the 'Clio's' Committee. It was also expected that every boy so nominated was physically fit for a sailor's life, had been approved by the Committee and Medical Officer, was willing to be bound down to remain on the 'Clio' for a certain period of time, and go to sea when a ship had been selected for him.

Members of the Association, who were annual subscribers of £1. 1s. and upwards, could nominate one boy for that amount. Life Governors had the privilege of nominating one boy for every £25 donated to the Society before the 30th June, 1877, and were only expected to subscribe an annual payment of £10 for each boy.

The period a boy was to remain on board the 'Clio', and the time he was to leave was to be determined by the Executive Committee subject to the control of the Secretary of State. The Society emphasised that under no circumstances would they accept on board the 'Clio' any boy who had been in prison.

CHAPTER 5

The rules and bye-laws regulating the constitution and management of the society governing the Industrial Training Ship 'Clio'

It was laid down that the Institution should be called 'The North Wales, City of Chester, and Border Counties Industrial School Training Ship Society'. The object of the Society was to receive and train for the sea 250 boys, towards whose maintenance some contribution should be guaranteed, as well as boys who through poverty, or parental neglect, were left without proper means of support, education, and control; who were to be admitted, fed and clothed in such a way that the General or Executive Committee would decide, subject to the approval of the Home Office under the powers of the Industrial Schools Act, 1866, and amending Acts.

Members of the Society would consist of Annual Subscribers of £1. 1s. and upwards, and of Life Governors, who were donors of £25 and upwards. Life Governors would have the privilege of nominating one boy between the ages of 11 and 15 for every £25 donated before the 30th June, 1877, and on an annual payment of £10 for each boy, subject to the approval of the Local and Executive Committees. Any member of the Society could nominate a boy on an annual payment of £20 for each boy. Annual subscriptions would be due in advance, on the 1st January every year.

The management of the Society was to be vested in the President, Vice-Presidents, Life Governors, a General, an

HMS Conway

Mr John Jones, teacher

The band

Boys with ship's pets

Rope craft

Capt. Langdon, Rev. S. Bradford with a group of the boys

Capt. Langdon, three lady visitors from U.S.A. with some of the boys

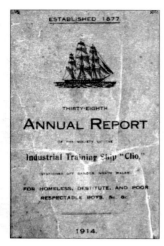

Cover Annual Report 1914

*Communal grave of boys –
Llandegfan*

Summer camp, Bodafon fields, Llandudno

The band Bangor railway station

The 'Clio' band leaving Bangor pier – Empire Day Parade

Mr Bates, bandmaster with his wife and two daughters

Captain Langdon and staff

Summer camp, Bodafon fields, Llandudno

Picnic, Glyn Garth, Anglesey

Chaplain – The Rev. S. Bradford

Signallers R.N.R. who joined 1914

Ship's concert party

Picnic at Bryn Mêl, Anglesey

The 'Clio' staff

Boat pulling instruction

The boys in bed

Boy as received

Same boy the day after

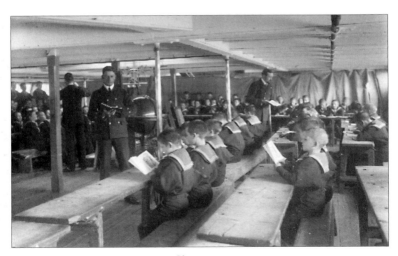

Class-room

*Ex member of staff visiting
the ship during W.W.I*

Stanley Conder

Cutlass drill

Shoe making with Mr Godfrey

Parade, Bodafon fields summer camp

Field gun's crews
summer camp

Instruction in masts and sail

Boys who joined the services 1914

Mr Godfrey – shoemaker

Dancing the hornpipe

Funeral Menai Bridge

The 'Clio' on her way to be broken up

Executive, and a Finance Committee, a Treasurer and a Secretary. The President, Treasurer and Secretary were to be '*ex-officio*' members of all the Committees. The General Committee would consist of donors of 10 gns. and upwards, annual subscribers of 2 gns. and upwards, and of the Vice-Presidents and Life Governors, who would be 'ex-officio' members of the General Committee. This General Committee was to meet on board the 'Clio' twice a year, in May and October, when they would inspect the ship and examine the boys. Five members of this committee would form a quorum.

The Executive Committee was to consist of not more than 24 members, which were to be elected from and by the General Committee, with power to appoint a Local and other Sub-Committees, and would meet for business at least once a quarter. Three members would form a quorum. One-third of the members of the Executive were to retire annually, but were eligible for re-election. The Finance Committee would consist of not more than 12 members, and would be elected from and by the Executive annually, but would be eligible for re-election.

The annual meeting of the Society would take place in January of every year, seven days notice being given. At the meeting they would receive reports and statement of account. Meetings for special purposes could be called by the President upon the requisition of five members of the General Committee, again with seven days notice being given.

The Executive Committee would have the power to appoint and discharge all officers and servants. With the consent of the Secretary of State, and confirmation of their proceedings by the General Committee the Executive would have the power to make, sanction, or alter the regulations for the management of the ship. They were also to see that proper books were kept on board to explain the management. These books were to be open for inspection by any member of the General, Executive or Local Committees. No outlay would be incurred without the consent of the Executive or Local Committee.

The Local Committee would be required to visit the ship once a quarter, and would appoint from among their body two people that would visit the ship each month. Each visiting member of this committee would have to visit the 'Clio' at least once during his term of office, with the purpose of seeing that the admissions were in accordance with the orders of the Executive Committee, and that the general arrangements for the management of the ship were properly carried out. On his last visit he would make an official report in the form provided by the Executive Committee. Any elected visitor unable to attend to his duties would have to procure a substitute from among the members of the Local or Executive Committee.

The Minutes of the proceedings of all meetings would be recorded in a book or books kept for that purpose.

The Treasurer would be required to keep his account with the Bankers appointed by the Executive, and would at every annual meeting of the Society 'exhibit a general statement of the pecuniary affairs' of the Institution, with detailed accounts of receipts and expenditure of the ship, which were to have been audited by a professional auditor, or audit committee, appointed by the Executive in the name of the Finance Committee and all cheques were to be signed by a member of the Finance Committee, and by the Secretary.

The Rules and Bye-Laws regulating the Management of the school stated that boys of all religious denominations would be eligible for admission to the 'Clio', on condition that they conform to the general rules and bye-laws relating to religious worship and instruction as conducted in the ship. These were; that each day should begin and end with the simple family worship (to be prescribed by the Local Committee) and the reading of the Bible. On Sunday the boys should attend public worship, either on board the ship, or at some convenient Church or Chapel. In the case of any boy admitted who was specified in the Order of Detention as being of some other religious denomination than the Church of England, a Minister of that denomination should be allowed to visit the boy, at such times and under such conditions that would be fixed and sanctioned by the Secretary of State. The boy should not be required to learn the catechism of the Church of England. The Sunday would be strictly observed and none but indispensable work should be performed on that day. It was stressed that it would be the duty of the Captain-Superintendent, and of the Officers, in the religious observance of the day, to make it a happy as well as an instructive day.

No boy would be received on board who, upon medical examination, was found to be unfit for a sailor's life. No boy under the age of 11 or above the age of 15 would be received on board except by special resolution of the Executive Committee. The period a boy would remain on board the 'Clio', and the time he would leave, were to be determined individually by the Executive Committee subject to the control of the Secretary of State.

The Captain-Superintendent was required to live on board, and it was his duty to see that all officers carried out their duties. He was expected to carry out all orders given to him by the Executive or Local Committee, at the same time he was to be responsible to both these committees for the good government of the ship, namely, the execution of all regulations, for the quantities and qualities of all supplies received on board, and for the proper application of such supplies. While enforcing strict discipline, he was expected to gain a 'salutory influence' over the boys individually, and by 'instilling into their minds Christian principles, seek to urge upon them the importance of leading a life of duty and usefulness.' Once a month he was to report in writing to the Local Committee on the state of the 'Clio', and attend to give personal explanations when required.

An additional part of the Captain-Superintendent's duties

were to keep a 'Register Book', in which was to be contained an account of the boys received and discharged from the 'Clio'; particulars of their previous history; of their conduct while on board; and as far as possible, their conduct after their discharge. A 'Log Book', in which was to be inserted everything of importance relating to the 'Clio', and to the discipline of the officers and boys. An 'Offence and Punishment Book' in which was to recorded particulars of all offences and the amount of punishment inflicted. A 'Conduct Book', which would record particulars of all badges and rewards for good conduct and application to study. A 'Cash Book', with particulars of all money received for or paid on account of the 'Clio' by the Captain-Superintendent. A 'General Order Book' in which was to be entered all new regulations communicated to him by the Secretary of the Society, copies of which were to be kept by the Secretary in a separate book. A 'Visitor's Book', and any other books the Executive or Local Committee would decide, or which the Secretary of State would require.

Authorisation was given to the Captain-Superintendent to punish the boys detained in the school in cases of misconduct. However, all offences and punishments were to be entered in the 'Offence and Punishment Book', which would in turn be laid before the Executive and Local Committees at their meetings. Punishments could consist of forfeiture of rewards and privileges, reduction in quality or quantity of food, confinement in a room or lighted cell for not more than three days, and 'MODERATE' personal correction not exceeding twelve strokes with a birch, rod or cane. It was essential, however, to see that when these punishments were carried out, that no child would be deprived of two meals in succession, that any boy in confinement should be allowed not less than one pound of bread and gruel, or milk and water daily. The more serious offences would be dealt with by the Executive or Local Committee. If any boy, sent to the 'Clio' under the provisions of the Industrial Schools Act, was found guilty of an offence for which any of the aforementioned punishments would appear inadequate, he would, by the permission of the Executive or Local Committee, be brought before the Magistrates, with a view to his being committed to a Reformatory or Prison, and his discharge from the school would be applied for to the Secretary of State as incorrigible.

The boys were to be supplied with 'plain wholesome food' according to a Dietary that would be approved of by an Inspector.

The parents or other relations or friends of the boys were allowed to correspond with them at 'reasonable times', and to visit them on board once in two months, on an appointed day, but such privileges were to be forfeited by misconduct or interference with the discipline of the School. A written application would have to be made to the Captain-Superintendent before each visit, and he would forward to the applicant a ticket specifying the time of such a visit.

All letters to or from the boys would be opened by the Captain-Superintendent, or his deputy, who would retain them if they appeared to be of an improper character, or from an improper person, and they would be passed on to the Secretary. The boys were prohibited from receiving any presents without the consent of the Captain-Superintendent.

No strangers would be admitted on board the 'Clio' without the permission of the Captain-Superintendent, or his authorised representative, should he be absent. No visitors were to be allowed on board on Sunday.

No officer or person belonging to the ship could receive any gratuity from the boys, their friends, visitors, tradespeople, or others. Anyone found accepting gratuities would be instantly dismissed. The Captain-Superintendent would have the power to suspend, for misconduct, any officer of the school pending the decision of the Local or Executive Committee.

One or more Medical Officer would be appointed by the Executive Committee, who would continue in office during the pleasure of that committee. A Medical Officer should visit the ship regularly, clear of meal hours, twice a week, and in the event of an illness as often as the case would require. He would personally examine all new boys, and once in three months examine all the boys 'stripped at divisions'. He was required to report to the Captain-Superintendent personally the boys' state of health after each visit, enter his visits, with a written report of any case of serious illness or disease, and the course of treatment prescribed, in a book kept for that purpose.

In the case of the sudden or violent death of any inmate of the school, an inquest would be held, and the circumstances of the case were to be reported immediately to the Inspector. The Inspector should also be informed immediately of any boy deserting from the school, dying while an inmate of the school, or being committed to a Reformatory.

The boys would be examined, and their proficiency in school instruction and industrial training tested from time to time by the Inspector of Reformatory and Industrial Schools. All books and journals of the school would be open to him for examination. Any teacher employed for the instruction of the boys could be examined by him, if he thought it necessary. He was to receive prior notice of the appointment or discharge of the Captain-Superintendent, and the Schoolmaster.

Three hours daily of secular instruction would consist of reading, spelling, writing, ciphering, vocal music, and as far as possible the elements of history, geography and drawing. The religious instruction would be in accordance with the principles of the Church of England, and would be given daily. Not less than five hours daily would be given over to industrial training, which was instruction in naval exercises and employments, and the elements of navigation. Two hours daily would be allowed for recreation and exercise. Once or twice a week, when practicable, the boys would be taken ashore for exercise, or they would have swimming lessons, 'when occasion and safety permitted', in charge of one or more officers of the ship. A time-table showing the hours of work, school instruction, meals, etc., as approved by the Inspector should be fixed in the school-room.

No boy would be allowed to go from, or sleep out of, the 'Clio' without the consent of the Captain-Superintendent, or his authorised representative, should he be absent.

Any boy discharged from the school would be provided with a sufficient outfit, according to the circumstances of the discharge, and should be apprenticed or placed out as far as practicable in 'some seafaring employment or service'. If a boy was returned to relatives or friends the expenses of such a return should be defrayed.

The officers and teachers would be required to maintain the discipline and order of the school, and to see to the instruction and training of the boys. Consequently, the boys would be expected to obey the officers and teachers, and to comply with the school regulations. Any boy who refused to obey the regulations, admitted under the provisions of the Industrial Schools Act 1866, could be classed as an offender under Section 32 of that Act.

The Schoolmaster was expected to supply the Captain with a quarterly report of the progress of the boys in school.

No boy would be permitted to retain money in his possession. Any money should be handed to the Captain-Superintendent, who would retain it for the benefit of the boy to whom it was given. The Captain-Superintendent, at his discretion, would allow the boy to spend the money, but would endeavour to encourage every boy to save and invest their money.

The Captain-Superintendent would keep a register of admissions and discharges, with particulars of the parentage, previous circumstances, etc., of each child admitted, and of the disposal of each child discharged. He would regularly send to the office of the Inspector of Reformatory and Industrial Schools (under cover to the Under Secretary of State for the Home Department), the returns and quarterly accounts required, and in the month of January each year, a full statement of receipts and expenditure of the school, for the past year, showing all debts and liabilities, and duly vouched by the Audotir or Audit Committee.

Basically, these were the foundations upon which the Society of the Industrial Training Ship 'Clio', for Homeless, Destitute and Poor Respectable Boys, were based. No alteration could be made to these rules and regulations, except at an annual meeting, or special meeting, of the General Committee, called for that purpose, subject to the sanction of the Secretary of State, pursuant to the provisions of the Industrial Schools Act, 1866. These rules and regulations had been examined by W. Inglis, Inspector of Reformatory and Industrial Schools, and approved on the 13th February, 1878, at Whitehall by R. Assheton Cross, Principal Secretary of State for the Home Department.

CHAPTER 6

1878 – The first year and teething troubles

At the end of the year 1877 there were 28 boys on board the 'Clio'. The *North Wales Chronicle* carried a weekly report of the new arrivals, and on the 19th January, 1878, proudly proclaimed that there were now 50 boys on board; 'There were six fresh arrivals yesterday. A boy is daily expected from Newtown, and there are several applications.' The following week the paper reported that there were 63 boys on board, and that there were several more en route.

Surprisingly, there were still some people who had doubts about the purpose of the 'Clio'. There was still a feeling that the 'Clio' was a Reformatory and a ship for young criminals. Unfortunately it was a stigma that persisted whilst the 'Clio' was in the Straits, and even years later on was carried over to the 'Conway', which is even more surprising. The *North Wales Chronicle* of the 9th February, 1878, was, therefore, forced to explain in print once again, that 'in view of recent misrepresentations, too much emphasis cannot be laid on the fact that the ship is intended solely for the reception and training of homeless and destitute boys unconvicted of crime.' By now there were 72 boys on board, and the paper was pleased to report that a concert in aid of funds was to be held at the St James's Hall, London.

At a meeting of the Bangor and Beaumaris Board of Guardians on Wednesday, 13th February, there were complaints by the managers of being unable to cope with the sick boys from the 'Clio'. Since the 'Clio' did not have its own infirmary, a case of Scarletina from the ship had been admitted to their infirmary. By the 23rd February the *North Wales Chronicle* was able to report that there had been no further cases of fever on board the 'Clio', and that the ship was now perfectly healthy.

In March the Manchester School Board voted £250 towards the expenses of the ship, and the Salford School Board gave £100. There were now 133 boys on board. The Bangor and Beaumaris Board of Guardians, however, were not satisfied with the system of sending boys with fever to their infirmary. Three boys with Scarletina had already been admitted to their fever ward, and the Chairman of the Board of Guardians suggested that the committee of the 'Clio' should purchase a small cottage nearer to the ship, which could receive boys suffering from infectious diseases. Capt. Verney, who was on the Board of Guardians Committee as well as being on the 'Clio's' Committee, thanked the Chairman for his suggestion, but assured them that the 'Clio' boys would not be a burden to the Guardians because the 'Clio' committee would pay for the boys' maintenance.

During April an appeal was made to the public for £50 to buy musical instruments for the Band that was to be established on the 'Clio'. Within a month the new instruments for the Band had arrived and practices were held daily. The 'Clio' Band was to become famous through the whole of North Wales, and during 1878 was given credit for giving Eisteddfod Gadeiriol Môn a much needed lift when it was held at Menai Bridge that year; the 'Clio' Band being one of the main attractions.

On the 19th June, the Band was to play at Baron Hill, Beaumaris, when Sir Richard and Lady Williams Bulkeley were going to throw open to visitors their private gardens and rosary for the benefit of the 'Clio' funds. Before then though, the 'Clio' was to receive a visit from Mr Henry Rogers, the Deputy Inspector of Industrial Schools.

Mr Rogers had very little to report. The ship had been certified on the 29th August, 1877. It was intended to meet the wants of North Wales, city of Chester and border counties, by training for sea service homeless and destitute boys from that district, and generally to provide nautical training and suitable instruction for children who could be sent to the ship under the provisions of the Industrial Schools Act, 1866. At the end of 1877, there had been 28 boys on board and that number had increased to 137 by March, 1878. The ship had been thoroughly fitted and prepared for the reception and training of boys for the sea, at a cost of more than £7,000, wholly contributed by private benevolence. A suitable staff of officers had been appointed, and the ordinary routine of an Industrial Training Ship had been duly established.

On Friday, 9th August 1878, the 'Clio' celebrated its first anniversary with a 'goodly gathering' on board the ship. To the landsman the 'Clio' appeared to be a marvel of good order and cleanliness; and even to the nautical eye the ship was without 'spot or blemish'; and it must have occurred to the minds of all who had the pleasure of being present that a home where everything was so well ordered could not but exercise a wonderful influence upon the habits of those who lived within its wooden walls, and who have left their nomadic life behind them. The visitors could not fail to be struck with the manifest contentment of the boys, and the cheerfulness which prevailed in their midst.

To entertain the visitors, the boys, after they marched around the deck, with the Brass Band at their head, were put through a variety of movements, which they executed with great precision. 'They presented a thoroughly sailor-like appearance, and their performances showed they had been most carefully drilled.' The Duke of Westminster, and others, addressed those gathered there, before his wife, the Duchess, presented the boys with their prizes. There were prizes for the most popular boy in the ship; the boy with the highest number of marks in each standard; the best tailor; the best shoe-maker; the best clothes; and prizes for seamanship.

Less than a fortnight following the first anniversary celebrations tragedy was to strike the 'Clio'. James Hemmett, aged eleven, fell from the yard-arm on Tuesday evening, the 20th August. He died at seven o'clock the following evening. An inquest was held at the Gazelle Inn on the Friday. Mr R. Jones-Roberts, the county coroner, and a jury, of which Mr Thomas Morgan was foreman, heard how James Hemmett had fallen from 65 to 70 feet from the yard-arm to his death. The jury returned a verdict of 'accidental death', and recommended that nets be placed under the yards while the boys were exercising aloft. The deceased had only been some five weeks on board the 'Clio', and came from the Manchester area. He was buried on the Saturday afternoon at Llandegfan Parish Churchyard.

CHAPTER 7

Daily routine on board the 'Clio'

The 'Clio' boys, once they had been admitted onto the ship, were divided into two Watches, Port and Starboard. The Starboard Watch had a distinguishable red stripe round their right sleeve, and the Port Watch had theirs round the left sleeve. Each boy was supplied with three suits of uniform – a working suit, a second best, and a best suit. These suits and underclothing were made on board by 'tailor-boys', who were paid for each article they made, and the sum handed over to them on their leaving the ship. All the boys' boots were also made on board.

The boys were summoned out of bed by a bugle call at 5.30 a.m. in summer and 6.00 a.m. in winter. The first out to bath were the 'bed-placers' and the petty-officer boys, who were distinguished by the badge of crossed anchors on their sleeves which had been gained for good conduct. There were ten baths supplied with hot and cold water. When the 'bed-placers' had performed their ablutions they returned to stow away the beds, while the main body retired below to the bath deck. At 6.30 a.m. the decks were cleaned, and at 7.15 a.m. the cooks for the day were sent to get the mess deck ready for breakfast. This was served at 7.30 a.m. and consisted of 5 ozs of oat-meal and half a pint of milk, or an 'ample meal of bread and cocoa'. At 8.00 a.m. a boat was despatched for the officers who came on duty for the day. After the wood and brasswork were cleaned the boys fell into divisions for inspection at 8.15 a.m. There were four divisions, with an officer in charge of each division. All officers were required to attend inspection. After a short drill, followed by prayers at 9.15 a.m. it was time to assemble for school at 9.30 a.m.

School was attended by one Watch at a time, morning and afternoon alternately, with the exception of the small and backward boys, who had to attend school all day. The Watch not at school attended technical instruction, or the 'industrial training' part of their education. This consisted of such things as boat-pulling, knots and splices, bends and hitches, signalling; both Morse and semaphore, boxing the compass, steering model, sailmaking, ship's model, swimming, tailoring, carpentry, shoemaking, gunnery (heavy guns and field guns), rifle practice, and Band practice. Unfortunately there is no detailed time-table of the industrial training given on board the 'Clio', but for the type of intensive training given on other ships of the period and of the same calibre as the 'Clio'.

From 11.00 a.m. until 11.15 a.m. the boys were on 'stand-easy', and then it was back to school until 12.30 p.m. Dinner, which usually consisted of meat, potatoes, and a suet pudding, was served at 1.00 p.m. After dinner the boys were at liberty to play about as much as they liked until school recommenced at 2.00 p.m. In the words of Charles E. B. Russell, it was the time when many a boy 'usually may be seen on the upper or hurricane decks enjoying himself to the top of his best'. At 2.00 p.m. the boys went to 'divisions' again, and the Watches were reversed. School continued until 4.30 p.m. with a break for 'stand-easy' from 3.15 p.m. to 3.30 p.m. According to Mr Russell, 'the rest of the evening, after a good tea, being spent in play, boat practice, or it may be drill. At 7.00 p.m. it is time for prayers, and at 8.00 p.m. all are once more safely in bed'.

Although Mr Russell is inclined to think that the period after dinner, most of the evenings were spent in play, the more detailed routine of the 'Exmouth' shows that it was not all play for the boys during this period. A similar routine was probably carried out on the 'Clio', when after dinner, Cooks were expected to wash-up, sweep out messes and clear up the mess deck.

The evening routine on the 'Exmouth', and there is little doubt that such a highly organised establishment as the 'Clio' did not have a similar routine, was as follows:

4.50 Captains and Cooks of messes.
5.00 Supper.
5.20 Cook of messes wash up. Letter boat. Fill up tanks and cisterns. Open lower deck parts.
6.00 Assembly. School Watch to school or singing; working Watch to seamanship; on Monday,
      Tuesday, Thursday and Friday; and on Wednesday and Saturday the Band plays for boys to
      dance.
6.44 Clear up decks.
6.45 Retreat. Open all parts.
7.35 Clear Decks. Open all parts. Take in spare lamps.
7.50 Assembly on Orlop deck, to stand-by hammocks.
      Sound one G - get up main deck hammocks.
      Sound two G's – get up lower deck hammocks.
      Sound three G's – get up Orlop deck hammocks.
8.00 Bed call. Prayers. Turn in. Rounds.
10.00 Officers' lights out.

The one perpetual complaint about the 'Clio's' daily routine was that the boys had very little opportunity to go ashore, either for walks or games. From the earliest days there were doubts about the position the 'Clio' had been moored at, and from some of the observations of the Chief Inspector it seemed that the boys had very little opportunity to even spend time on the decks to get some exercise in the fresh air, especially during the winter months. 'The present position of the ship, however, is one of great exposure to wind and tide. The officers represent that in bad weather the risk is excessive, and access to ship and shore difficult and dangerous for boats' crews composed of very young boys.'

In his fourth Annual Report Captain Moger stated that he had to ask for a sub-committee to be formed to enquire into the desirability of removing the ship to a more sheltered anchorage, as he considered the ship's position to be too exposed and unsafe in very bad weather. Following the death of one of the boys from pneumonia, and another boy ending up suffering from an acute case of rheumatism during the winter of 1880, the Chief Inspector still complained that the ship's situation was 'cold and exposed' and that the boys needed the 'utmost protection from wind and weather'. However, nothing was done to alleviate the situation, and the Chief Inspector following his inspection on the 27th May, 1882, still maintained that the situation was stormy and exposed, 'too much so for the class of boys dealt with. They need every possible protection from the stiff gales and strong seas they have to battle with'. No wonder he reported that the 'boys looked hardy and seasoned'. By 1886, a new covered play-deck had been added, giving the boys complete protection from the weather, although by this time it appeared that the boys had become 'injured to exposure and thrive and keep well'.

The new swimming bath at Bangor was being made good use of by the turn of the century and the majority of the boys could swim. The boys were also by now 'occasionally landed for play and walks'. The following year the Chief Inspector was happy to report that 'the great step in advance during the year has been the hiring of a play field on shore. This is a most valuable auxiliary to a stationary ship, and the change ashore should improve the health on board'.

There is little information concerning the ship's routine on

Saturdays and Sundays. 'Two ladies and some other friends in the neighbourhood give the boys an occasional treat.' The *North Wales Chronicle* of the period is full of reports of Fetes, Picnics, Parades and Eisteddfodau attended by the 'Clio' board. The local gentry made full use of the 'Clio' boys on their open days. 'The private grounds of Baron Hill, Beaumaris, were opened to the public on 31st August (1886). The boys present went through various performances. About £15 was raised in aid of funds and the boys enjoyed themselves very much.' The following year 'by kind permission of Lady Augusta Mostyn, the private grounds of Gloddaeth were opened to the public on 21st September (1887). The boys were present and went through various exercises. About £12 was realised in aid of funds, and the boys enjoyed themselves very much.

There was also the yearly pilgrimage to Chester for the Annual General Meeting at the Town Hall, Chester, when the boys travelled from Bangor to Chester by train. From Chester Station they marched to the Town Hall, with the 'Clio' Band at the head of the procession. The boys travelled as far afield as Wolverhampton, when on Saturday, 22nd August, 1903, a detachment of boys from the 'Clio' took part in the Wolverhampton Lifeboat Saturday Fund Parade. A fortnight later they were leading the parade at Bangor when Baden-Powell was given the Freedom of the Borough. The boys were rewarded by the great man paying their ship a visit. The found of the Boy Scouts movement gave them a 'stirring address', which ended with the advice of 'carry out your orders at all costs even if you are killed in doing so'. Advice which many of the 'Clio' boys were to follow to the letter, with the Great War of 1914-18 looming on the horizon.

On Sundays the boys attended for morning service at Bangor Cathedral or St Mary's Church, Deiniol Road. St Mary's Church was the ship's Church, where many of the boys were baptised and confirmed. The highlight of the day was the service on board ship in the evening, which was attended by many local people. As one A.F.L. was to write in the 'Missions to Seamen Magazine', 'We should not miss the opportunity of being aboard for a Sunday Service if we would know one of the happiest features of Training Ship life. The singing of such hymns as 'Fight the good fight' or 'Fierce raged the tempest' by two or three hundred hearty, tuneful voices, led, perhaps, by the ship's band, is something one will not easily forget.

And then there is a brief straight 'yarn' from the Chaplain, and the sight of those faces, all intent of the menage he is to give, will, at one and the same time, fill his heart with humility and inspiration – humility as he thinks of his own inability in face of the great mission that has been given to him and inspiration as he devotes himself anew to the Father in Heaven for His service among those so young.

And be sure that the lads UNDERSTAND. They know the meaning of a true spiritual life, and they take their Confirmation as a real thing – a pledge of loyalty to their King Jesus – and are ready to listen to a bit of serious talk.

During the summer the boys were taken to Camp at Llandudno. They were conveyed there free of charge by the North Wales Steamship Company, 'with their usual generosity'. The boys camped in Bodafon Fields, Craig-y-don, and 'whilst there, the boys had several treats and entertainments, and had their annual exhibition of drill and sports'. It was a time which the 'Clio' boys looked forward to and also the people of Llandudno, as one admirer was to write to the local press, 'It does my heart good to see these beautifully trained boys marching into the town. They are a credit to their ship and to the men who have had the training of them'.

Many Industrial and Reformatory Schools had a small auxiliary home at the seaside to which the children could be sent to in batches, others hired a large empty house, which could be obtained cheaply early or late in the season. A large number of the boys' schools, such as the 'Clio', simply went in for a camp life. The 'Bradford Observer' describes in detail the Calder Farm Reformatory, Yorkshire, camp under the title 'A Reformatory Encampment at Mirfield'. The value of this change of air did not only have a direct affect on the children's health, it enabled the school buildings or the ship to have the rest 'which they need as much as persons'. It afforded an opportunity to thoroughly cleanse, air, and sweeten the establishment, whilst at the same time affording 'a wholesome break in a routine, which might if too long persisted in having a dulling effect upon children who have not like ordinary children homes to which they can go for their holidays'.

CHAPTER 8

School time table and curriculum

Although it was generally accepted that the education and industrial training given to the inmates of the 'Clio' was sufficient to ensure that they were accepted in the Mercantile Marine, it fell well below the standard for acceptance in the Royal Navy, except for the period of the Great War, 1914-18, when not unnaturally many of the 'Clio' boys enlisted.

The 'conditions of entry' as laid down by the Admiralty were that, 'a boy **must** be of good character, and able to read and write'. The lowest test was the ability to read a passage from a Standard II Reading Book (New Code), to write a passage dictated from the same book, and to sign his name. The original hope that the Industrial Training Ships were to be the main suppliers of personnel for sea service, both for the Mercantile and Royal Navy, was not bearing fruit. In his Report for 1896, the Chief Inspector listed that out of a total of 70 boys discharged from the 'Clio' during the year, only 31 actually went to sea. The difficulties in the way of 'disposing' boys to the sea were many. In the first place, many boys showed little interest in following a career afloat. Many parents were against their boys joining a ship, as they felt there was a greater need for them to be at home to supplement the parents meagre wages. A large number of boys were not physically fit to follow a life afloat, and there was also the necessity, in certain classes of sea employment, of finding money for a premium. The Royal Navy's 'Conditions of Entry', barred many of the Industrial School Ship boys from joining, except for the

Band boys, who were also welcomed in the Army. The Industrial Training Ship boy was not excluded from the Royal Navy, but neither was he welcomed, mainly because of his past history and upbringing. Consequently, it meant that 'the most powerful stimulus to stir the imagination of a boy on one of the Industrial Training Ships, viz., the hope of one day entering the Royal Navy, which is to boys the highest embodiment of sea life, is of small avail'.

The system of training boys for the sea was not working as it should, simply because the majority of boys committed to these ships were from the slums of the great cities. Not unnaturally these boys probably liked the slums and the excitement of a town life. The authorities found that they could not do as they liked with a boy once they had admitted him to a Training Ship. If a boy did not wish to go to sea, the authorities could send him to sea for a single sea voyage whilst under 16 years of age, but once he had attained the age of 16 he could walk ashore and it had 'not yet been suggested that there should be some agency in the nature of a press gang to seize him and carry him on board another ship to force him to make another voyage'.

The essential service performed by the Industrial School Ships was not that they took for a few months boys whose hearts were set on a sea life, but that they took boys from the streets without any peculiar love or even knowledge of the sea, and in the course of a few years by familiarising them with the various aspects of a sailor's life instil into them a desire to adopt it. Whilst doing this, they were also expected to educate them in the basic subjects children were taught in the ordinary schools.

The Classes or Standards in the 'Clio', as in the other Training Ships, were the same as those laid down by the Board of Education in their School Code for Elementary Schools in England and Wales. Basically, there were by these regulations six standards of proficiency, beginning with Standard I, which was of the most elementary character, requiring but the slightest knowledge of what has become known as the 3 R's.

Watch	Days	Classes	A.M. 9.30 to 11.00	A.M. 11.15 to 12.30		P.M. 2.00 to 3.15	P.M. 3.30 to 4.30
STARBOARD	MONDAY	1	Reading and Spelling	Arithmetic Tables		Dictation and Reading	Spelling
		2	Arithmetic	Dictation		Reading	Transcription
		3	Writing	Reading		Dictation	Spelling
		4	Arithmetic	Dictation		Reading	Geography
		5	Arithmetic	Reading		Writing	Geography
PORT	TUESDAY	1	Reading and Spelling	Dictation	Recreation and Dinner. From 12.30 to 2.00 p.m.	Arithmetic Tables	Dictation and Spelling
		2	Dictation	Arithmetic		Reading	Transcription
		3	Spelling	Dictation		Writing	Reading
		4	Arithmetic	Reading		Dictation	Geography
		5	Arithmetic	Reading		Dictation	Geography
STARBOARD	WEDNESDAY	1	Dictation	Arithmetic		Reading	Spelling
		2	Arithmetic	Spelling		Transcription	Dictation
		3	Reading and Spelling	Dictation		Arithmetic	Geography and Tables
		4	Writing and Arithmetic	Dictation		Reading	Spelling
		5	Arithmetic	Reading		Dictation	Geography
PORT	THURSDAY	1	Writing and Arithmetic	Reading and Spelling		Writing	Dictation
		2	Reading	Transcription		Arithmetic Tables	Geography
		3	Arithmetic	Geography		Writing	Spelling
		4	Dictation	Reading		Arithmetic	Writing
		5	Dictation	Geography		Writing	Geography
STARBOARD	FRIDAY	1	Reading and Arithmetic	Spelling and Writing		Dictation and Tables	)
		2	Reading	Dictation		Transcription	)
		3	Arithmetic	Geography		Tables and Spelling	)
		4	Dictation	Reading		Writing	)
		5	Arithmetic	Dictation		Writing	)

SUNDAYS: 3.00 to 4.00 p.m. - Religious Instruction

SCHOOL TIME SHEET

From 'Third Annual Report of the Industrial Training Ship 'Clio' '
1879, p. 34

Standard I were expected to be able to read a short paragraph from a book, not confined to words of one syllable. They were expected to copy in manuscript character a line of print, 'on slates or in copy-books, at choice of Managers', and write from dictation a few common words. In Arithmetic they were expected to notate and numerate up to 1,000. Do simple addition and subtraction of numbers of not more than four figures, and know the multiplication table to 6 times 12.

Standard II were expected to read with intelligence a short paragraph from an elementary reading book. Write a sentence from the same book, slowly read once, and then dictated. To point out the nouns in the passages read or written. Notate and numerate up to 100,000, and know the four simple rules of addition, subtraction, multiplication and division, up to and including short division. In Geography they were expected to know the definitions, points of compass, form and motion of the earth, and the meaning of a map.

By the time they reached Standard III they were expected to read with intelligence a short paragraph from a more advanced reading book. Write a sentence slowly dictated from the same book, and point out the nouns, verbs and adjectives. The Inspector would also examine the children's copy-books – 'small hand, capital letters and figures'. In Arithmetic they were now expected to be able to notate and numerate up to 1,000,000, do long division, and compound addition and subtraction of money. They were expected to know the outlines of the geography of England with special knowledge of the county in which the school was situated.

Standard IV were expected to read with intelligence a few lines of prose or poetry selected by the Inspector. Write eight lines slowly dictated from a reading book and parse a simple sentence. Copy books were again to be inspected and were to show an improvement in 'small hand'. In Arithmetic, compound rules (money) and reduction (common weights and measures) were expected to have been mastered. The children were further examined in the outlines of the geography of Great Britain, Ireland and the Colonies, and the outlines of the history of England up to the time of the Norman Conquest.

The children in Standard V were to show improved reading ability, write from memory the substance of a short story read out twice, with marks given for handwriting, spelling and grammar. They were also expected to parse with analysis a 'simple' sentence. Show practice in Arithmetic with knowledge of 'bills of parcels' and simple proportion. In Geography they were expected to know the outlines of the geography of Europe, both physically and politically, whilst in History they should be able to answer questions on the history of England from the Norman Conquest to the Accession of Henry VII.

By the time the children reached Standard VI they should be reading with fluency and expression, capable of writing a short theme or letter, spelling grammar, handwriting and the composition of which would be taken into consideration when marking. Parsing and analysis of a short 'complex' sentence was expected, and in Arithmetic, knowledge of proportion, vulgar and decimal fractions. In Geography, the outlines of the geography of the world, and in History, the outlines of the history of England from Henry VII to the death of George III.

The above then was not an unreasonable standard of education to be achieved, especially when we compare it to the course of instruction given at the Naval Training School 'The Circe'. The following was the course of instruction:-

First Instruction – Lower School
Reading and writing from dictation.
Arithmetic as far as multiplication.

Second Instruction – Lower School
Reading and writing from dictation.
Arithmetic as far as reduction.

Third Instruction – Upper School
Reading and writing from dictation.
Arithmetic as far as fractions.
Geography.

Fourth Instruction – Upper School
Reading and writing from dictation.
Arithmetic, to include decimals.
Geography.

The above, by itself, does not convey much, until one sees the Standard each 'instruction' was expected to attain by the July examination of each year.

First Instruction – Lower School
1. Express in words 29047.
2. Express in figures fifty-eight thousand seven hundred and five.
3. Add together   9281
                      87369
                      546978
                      295437
                      88521
                      4756
4. From   7932184
   Take   6495837
5. Write out the multiplication table of 4 and 9 times.
6. Divide 9214672 by 7.
Write out an account of our Lord's visit to Jerusalem when a boy.

Second Instruction – Lower School
1. Divide 721493 by 97.
2. A man pays away £47.12s.4½d., £95.16s.11¾d., £125.0s.10¼d., £217.15s.6¾d., and £29.10s.3½d., how much does he pay altogether?

3. From   £14,167.10s.1¼d.
   Take   £9,284.12s.7½d.
4. Multiply £876.13s.6¾d. by 75
5. How many £ s d are there in one million threepences?
6. Reduce £360.17s.4½d. to half pence.

Write out the Apostle's Creed and an account of the promise of the birth of our Saviour.

Third Instruction – Upper School

Arithmetic:

1. On Monday there was received into the Bank of England 120 lbs. 10 ozs. 15 dwt. 20 gr. of gold; on
   Tuesday, 175 lbs. 9 ozs. 10 dwt., on Wednesday, 75 lbs. 6 ozs. 17 dwt. 21 gr., on Thursday 207 lbs. 11
   ozs. 18 dwt. 14 gr.; and on Friday, 143 lbs. 4 ozs. and 12 dwt.; how much was received altogether?
2. Multiply 10 weeks 6 days 18 hours 20 minutes by 98.
3. Divide 2,400yds. 3 grs. 2 nls. by 76.
4. If a bullock weighs 5 cwt. 2 qrs. 10 lbs., how many of the same weight would it take to weigh 27 tons.
   18 cwt. 3 qrs. 20 lbs?
5. How many miles, etc., are there in two hundred thousand four hundred and seventy-four yards?

Religious Knowledge and Geography

1. Write a biography of Joseph.
2. Describe the healing of the lame man at the gate of the temple.

1. Define and estuary, a headland, a tributary. Name three of each in England.
2. Coasting from Dover to Newcastle, in what general directions will the ships' course be? Mention the counties and chief seaport towns passed.

Fourth Instruction – Upper School

Arithmetic:
1. Divide 19$\underline{21}$ by 41
    $\overline{22}$
2. Multiply 4.063 by 1.02.
3. What is the value of .9375 of a cwt.?
4. Find by practice the value of 5,614 articles, at £3.12s.3½d. each.
5. Find by practice the value of 21 yds. 3 quarters 3 nails, at £1.16s.5¾d. per yard.
6. If 5 men build a boat in 10½ days, in what time would 21 men do it?
7. If 18 horses can carry away 4,500 cwt. of ammunition in 6 days, in what time could 108 horses carry away 90,000 cwt.?

Religious Knowledge and Geography
1. In St Luke, third chapter, the following persons are mentioned: Tiberius, Caiaphas, John, Esaias and Abraham. State briefly who these persons were.
2. Give our Lord's explanation of his parable of the sower.

Geography
1. Name the principal harbours and anchorages used by our ships belonging to the Mediterranean fleet.
2. Draw a map of England south of the Humber.

These actual questions set in the examination papers immediately reveal that the work was of a much higher and more advanced character than that which would be expected of a candidate sitting for the present day Certificate of Secondary Education or the General Certificate of Education examinations. As an example of our present day standards the C.S.E. Mathematics (Paper 1) 1970 asked:

1. What is the next number in the series? $\frac{1}{3}$ $\frac{2}{5}$ $\frac{3}{7}$ $\frac{4}{9}$ __

2. From the numbers 31 to 39 inclusive write down:
    i)   a number which is a perfect square __
    ii) a number which can be written as 2^5 __
    iii) a number which when divided by 7 gives a remainder of 5.[1C]

In the G.C.E. English Language Paper for 1970 candidates were asked to write about 500-600 words on ten topics ranging from:

a) It will be great relief when your 'O' levels are over and you are free to relax. Imagine what might be a perfect way to celebrate.

    To:

b) Continue one of the following as a true or imaginary account concerning yourself:
    i)   I could not believe it when I was chosen to . . .
    ii) We never did find out what became of . . .
    iii) If I could live that day again I am sure that I . . .

In Question 2 candidates were asked to read a passage from a short story called 'The Simple Life', and answer 10 questions on the text. Question 3, again, was the reading of a passage, with three questions to be answered on the passage. Question 4 required the candidate to write a letter to a friend or a speech to be delivered at their parents' wedding anniversary. There is no mention of grammar, sentence formation, spelling or standard of handwriting.

As a matter of further interest, Gwilym Evans quotes the following examples from the Entrance Scholarship Examination in Caernarfonshire in the early 1900s, and states that 'most of the questions set are equivalent in degree of difficulty to those set nowadays in the second and third year form Grammar School examinations.

1. Analyse fully:

a) Many people who saw the ship start said that she was not seaworthy and that they feared she might go down.
b) The boys climbing the tree broke the branch.
c) I must have dropped my purse getting into the train.
d) Consider the lilies of the field.

2. Correct the following, giving reasons for the corrections:

a) He ran as quick as he could to the doctor.
b) Neither of the boys have confessed or said they are sorry.
c) He is one of those men who says exactly what they think.

3. Give the objective case of: I, she, it, they, thou, you, he, we, myself, who.

Write down the present and past participles of: dig, sweep, eat, walk, hoe, raise.

4. Write five short sentences containing the word round as:

a) an adjective
b) a preposition
c) an adverb
d) a verb
e) a noun.

5. State (giving your reason in each case) to what part of speech each word in the following sentence belongs: 'England expects every man this day to do his duty.'

Mr Evans gives further examples from the Arithmetic paper in the 1902 examination:

2. Arrange the following fractions in order of magnitude beginning with the greatest:

.4476; $\dfrac{193}{431}$; .4478; $\dfrac{64}{143}$

5. The price of a quantity of coal, weighing 3½ tons is £4.12s.9d. If it be divided into two portions, one of which weighs 1 ton 8 cwt. 3 qrs find to the nearest penny the price which should be paid for each portion.

7. The first class is 2d. per mile and the second class is 1¼d. per mile. A and B travel the same distance – A first class; and B second class. A pays £1.11s.3d. more than B. What is the distance travelled?

8a. For boys only: A courtyard which measures 8 yards long and 6 yards 2ft. 6ins. wide is paved with tiles, each tile being a square 8 ins. wide. Find the cost of paving if the tiles cost £2.1s.8d. per 1000 and the bricklayer charges 6¾d. per square yard for his work.

b. For girls only: An equal number, half crowns and pence amount to £19.3s.11d. What is the number?

In the Industrial Training Ships the qualifications for passing from Class to Class, as given in the 'Exmouth' regulations were as follows:-

To pass from fifth into fourth class: You must be able to spell words of one syllable. Write a line on your slate from a copy. Do simple addition and subtraction sums, of not less than four figures, and know the multiplication table as far as '6 times 12'.

To pass from fourth into third class: You must be able to read a short paragraph from a book not confined to words of one syllable. To write a line of print on your slates or in copy-books; to write a few common words from dictation. Do simple addition and subtraction sums, and know the multiplication table to '6 times 12'. Standard I.

To pass from third into second class: You must read with intelligence a short paragraph from your reading-book. Write a sentence from the same book, slowly read once, and then dictated. Copy-books are to be shown. Work the four simple rules in arithmetic as far as short division. Point out the nouns in grammar, and answer easy questions in geography. Standard II.

To pass from second into first class: You must read with intelligence a short paragraph from your reader. Write a sentence from the same book, slowly dictated once. Show copy-books. Work simple long division and compound addition and subtraction (money sums). Point out nouns, verbs and adjectives. Answer questions upon the map of England, and the county of Essex. Standard III.

To pass out of school: You must read with intelligence a few lines of prose or poetry. Write eight lines of dictation from your reading-book. Show copy-books (small hand). Work all compound rules in arithmetic, together with reduction (weights and measures). Parse a simple sentence. Answer questions upon the geography of Great Britain, Ireland and the colonies; and also in English history. Standard IV.

All together a fairly comprehensive standard of education to be achieved with the 'wastrels of society', and the 'street Arabs'. In addition to this, these boys were expected to have a wide knowledge of seamanship, but more of that in the next chapter.

In his report for the year 1895, the Chief Inspector wanted it understood that in the Reformatories and Industrial Training Schools 'they were really working up in elementary and class subjects to the standard of ordinary elementary schools'. He goes on to give his views on the standard expected following the introduction of the new 'Code' of 1895, in Arithmetic, word-building, object lessons, Domestic Economy and Recitation.

The Inspector in his report for 1896, was in many ways paving the way for the standards to be achieved in the present day C.S.E. examinations. He believed that stress should be laid on the elder children in the Home Office schools to 'get in the way of reading, not only for the sake of reading itself, but also for the sake, and with an intelligent appreciation, of the subject-matter of the reading book'. He further advocated that 'the older children as they leave the schools shall be able to write a decent piece of simple composition, and it is hoped that by laying more stress on the body of the composition and the graphic presentment of it than upon the mere grammatical skeleton, this will be gained without composition being taught as an ordinary set subject. The point of view from which composition should be regarded in these schools is not that of grammar or punctuation, but of general intelligence'. In order that a clear view of what was actually being taught in the Home Office schools he gave two specimen schemes of work that had been sanctioned the previous year (1895). One is a scheme of work for a Farm School and the other for a Town School. A further scheme of work as carried out at the Kebble Institution is given in the Chief Inspector's Report for 1898.

By the outbreak of the First World War many Education Acts had been passed through Parliament, the methods and techniques of teaching had changed, and the 'Clio' school time-table had also changed its format, as we can see above. The Rules and By-Laws regulating the constitution and management of the 'Clio' quoted in their Thirty-Eighth Annual Report states that 'The secular instruction of the boys shall consist of reading, spelling, writing, cyphering, vocal music, and as far as practicable, the elements of history, geography, and drawing. It shall be given for three hours daily. The religious instruction shall be in accordance with the principles of the Church of England, and shall be given daily. The industrial education shall be instruction in naval exercises and employments, and the elements of navigation. The boys shall be employed in industrial work for not less than five hours daily'.

The Chief Inspector's 59th Annual Report (1916) showed his concern about schools that had their staffs deplated 'in some cases even to vanishing point', and although he found it impossible to criticise, as in normal times, the general standard of schoolroom work, he could not help expressing a fear 'that unless care be taken the standard of work in some schools may slip back more than is really excusable at the present time'. The Chief Inspector's main concern for this year was that many of the Gils' Schools were employing little girls to an excessive extent upon heavy household work such as scrubbing and cleaning floors, 'work fitted for a strong healthy charwoman, but not at all suitable for the little child for whom the Industrial School is supposed to take the place of home, but for whom I have sometimes a qualm that it becomes the above of soul-less drudgery'.

With the declaration of peace in 1918, the Home Office, following the Board of Education's example turned their thoughts to schemes of reconstruction and 'especially to schemes for the better upbringing of the coming generation', by producing a Circular Letter from H. M. Chief Inspector of Reformatory and Industrial Schools, to the Managers and Staff

Time Table from Thirty Eighth Annual Report of the Training Ship 'Clio', 1914, p. 61.

9–9.15: Spelling and Mental Arithmetic (all groups). Group column: Religious Instruction (all groups).
12.30–2.00 Recreation and Dinner.

Day	Station	Group	9.15–10.15	10.15–11.00	11.15–11.50	11.50–12.30	2.00–2.50	Station	2.50–3.40	3.40–4.30
Monday	Star-board	Junior	Arithmetic	Reading	Composition	History	Drawing	Port	Drawing	Recitation
		Inter., Senior	" "	Composition	Reading	English	" "		" "	" "
Tuesday	Port	Junior	Arithmetic	Reading	Dictation	Geography	Drawing	Star-board	Drawing	Recitation
		Inter., Senior	" "	Composition	Navigation	Reading	" "		" "	" "
Wednesday	Starboard	Junior	Arithmetic	Reading	Composition	Object Lesson Earth Knowledge Mensuration	Mental Arithmetic	Port	Composition	History
		Inter., Senior	" "	Composition	Science		" "		" "	Geography
Thursday	Port	Junior	Arithmetic	Reading	Dictation	Object Lesson Earth Knowledge Geography	Arithmetic	Starboard	Reading	Object Lesson Earth Knowledge Mensuration
		Inter., Senior	" "	Composition	Reading		Composition		Navigation	
Friday	Star-board	Junior	Arithmetic	Reading	Composition	Geography	History	Port	Reading	Geography
		Inter., Senior	" "	Composition	Navigation	" "	Reading		Geography	Revision

98

of the Schools. Four paragraphs from the Introduction to the Code of the Board of Education were quoted in the letter emphasising the aims the 'workers' in Home Office Schools, like their colleagues in the Public Elementary Schools were aiming for. That 'the purpose of the Public Elementary School is to form and strengthen the character and to develop the intelligence of the children entrusted to it, and to make the best use of the school years available, in assisting both girls and boys, according to their different needs, to fit themselves practically as well as intellectually for the work of life.

With this purpose in view it will be the aim of the School to train the children carefully in habits of observation and clear reasoning, so that they may gain an intelligent acquaintance with some of the facts and laws of nature, to arouse in them a living interest in the ideals and achievements of mankind, and to bring them to some familiarity with the literature and history of their own country; to give them some power over language as an instrument of thought and expression, and, while making them conscious of the limitations of their knowledge, to develop in them such a taste for good reading and thoughtful study as will enable them to increase that knowledge in after years by their own efforts.

The School must at the same time encourage to the utmost the children's natural activities of hand and eye by suitable forms of practical work and manual instruction; and afford them every opportunity for the healthy development of their bodies, not only by training them in appropriate physical exercises and encouraging them in organised games, but also by instructing them in the working of some of the simpler laws of health...

And, though their opportunities are but brief, the teachers can yet do much to lay the foundations of conduct. They can endeavour, by example and influence, aided by the sense of discipline which should prevade the School, to implant in the children habits of industry, self-control, and courageous perseverance in the face of difficulties; they can teach them to reverence what is noble, to be ready for self-sacrifice, and to strive their utmost after purity and truth; they can foster a strong sense of duty, and instil in them that consideration and respect for others which must be the foundation of unselfishness and the true basis of all good manners; while the corporate life of the School, especially in the playground, should develop the instinct for fair play and for loyalty to one another which is the germ of a wider sense of honour in later life'.

How far could Reformatory and Industrial Schools attain towards these ideals? It was felt that the children entered the Home Office Schools with many distinct disadvantages, but that they had exceptional opportunities for countering the disadvantages caused by early neglect and bad surroundings. The fact that the schools were residential gave the Superintendent and the teachers opportunities 'of which their colleagues in Day Schools may well be envious'. The Chief Inspector believed that 'the whole life of the child is subject to the tutelage of the School, and it is in the power of the School Staff to guide the education which goes on all day, weekdays and Sundays, not only with the book or pen, but in the workshop, the hobby room, the playing field, the garden, the farm, at meals, and in the holiday camp. The Reformatory and Industrial School is the child's home, classroom, playground, and in many cases, place of worship. The Superintendent can dispose of the child's whole time during several impressionable years. He and his staff can mound the little world from which the child will derive his conceptions of society, of manners, of conduct, of knowledge and of religions'. Theoretically, at least, the Home Office Schools had the ideal opportunity to produce the perfect members of society from what had originally been the 'wastrels of society' and the 'seething mass at the foot of the social ladder'.

The fact that the 1918 Education Act abolished the old provisions under which children might spend half time at work and half time at school, and required that all children under 14 (or 15 if the Local Education Authority fixed this higher age) should attend school full time, were to prove a problem as regards industrial training. Although these provisions did not extend to children in Reformatory and Industrial Schools, it was clearly incumbent on the Managers of these schools to see that the children under their care were no worse off than other children. The main defects of the Home Office schools had been that the children spent too much time in occupations which, though not necessarily bad in themselves, prevented the child spending his time and energies in ways that were educationally better. The object of restricting the employment of children was to secure that the child while in school should profit to the full from the education provided. The Chief Inspector believed that 'This consideration is as applicable to the children in Home Office Schools as to other children and we must bear in mind that though employment or useful work (at proper times and properly restricted) is good, it is bad if it encroaches on the time that should be given to organised training or healthy recreation'.

The feeling of the time was based on Dewey's philosophy of education. 'Personality, character, is more than subject-matter. Not Knowledge or information, but self-realization, is the goal.' There was a need for the better co-ordination of all parts of the curriculum. 'All sides of the school life should be organised with a view to the education of the child.' The man in charge of the workshops, the farm bailiff who shows a lad how to plough or insists on cleanliness in the byre, the laundry matron, the cook, the drill instructor, the bandmaster, should all be co-operators with the schoolroom teacher in developing the child's powers of observation and reasoning, in training his hands and eyes, and in moulding his ideas of conduct.'

In many schools some of these recommendations had been carried out, but there were still schools where drastic reorganisation and the employment of more adult assistance would be needed to do the necessary work of the institution. The Chief Inspector foresaw that the greatest changes would have to be in the organisation of the farm schools. 'In Industrial Schools especially it will be necessary either to reduce the farming operations or to engage adults to do much of the work.' From this statement one wonders whether the so called industrial training part of the education in some schools was truly industrial training or a disguised form of child labour?

The Dewey philosophy of educating the child, and 'it is he and not the subject-matter which determines both the quality and quantity of learning', and its consequent influence on Fisher's 1918 Education Act spelt the beginning of the end for the Industrial Training Schools. They were no longer to be 'the means of supplying the navy' or of solving the problem of the 'street-Arabs'. The Chief Inspector, Mr Arthur H. Norris, was of the opinion however, that 'the record of the Schools in the past is a testimony to the earnest desire of the Managers and officers to give to the boys and girls entrusted to their care the best possible change of making up for the neglect and disadvantages which lead to their commital', and it was with a view to a fuller realisation of this ideal that he had made the recommendations in the form of a letter to the Managers and Staff of the Reformatory and Industrial Schools.

CHAPTER 9
Training for the Sea

As has been previously noted, the purpose of the Industrial Schools was not only to solve the problem of the 'street-Arabs' by educating them, but to prepare them for industry, as in the case of the 'Clio', for a seafaring life.

The seamanship instruction in the 'Clio', as in other ships, was given under men who as a rule had served their time for pension in the navy as petty officers, or who had nearly finished such time, and were allowed to complete that time in the training ships as instructors. Half the time allocated for 'schooling' was given over to industrial training. On the 'Clio', in the morning, whilst the Starboard Watch were in the schoolroom, the Port Watch were having seamanship instruction. This process was reversed in the afternoon, so that both Watches ended up having the same amount of schooling and seamanship instruction.

The Chief Inspector of Reformatory and Industrial Schools when inspecting the ship, not only examined the boys in the schoolroom, but also in industrial training. Following his inspection of the 'Clio' on the 26th May, 1880, the Chief Inspector gives his first detailed report on the industrial training given as follows: 'The nautical training and exercises are very carefully and practically attended to. Instructions were going on on the rule of the road, lifesaving apparatus, signal code, sail making, canvas bag making, fender making, knotting, splicing and slinging, etc. There is a tailoring class and a class for repairing shoes. The boys were getting on well, and took interest in their occupations and technical instructions; gunnery instruction is also provided for.'

Unfortunately there is no time-table of the 'Clio's' seamanship classes available, but it would probably have followed the same pattern as that laid down for the 'Exmouth', which is given in full in Appendix 16.

The instructions given in seamanship were quite intensive, consisting of learning the names and being able to point out the parts of a ship, ship's fittings, masts and yards, standing rigging and sails, in addition to working out various exercises on the monkey topsail-yard. Boys were expected to name, use, and be able to make various bends and hitches, knots and splices, fully understand the compass and the use of the lead line. The subjects of instruction for the gunnery ships 'Excellent' and 'Cambridge' are given in full in Appendix 16.

On the 'Exmouth', to pass from one class to another in seamanship the boys had to know and understand the following:

To pass from fifth into fourth class: Must have a slight knowledge of names of spars and rigging, boat-duty, making clothes stops, washing and mending clothes, compass, lead and line, hammock drill, coiling ropes, bends, and hitches, and general information.

To pass from fourth into third class: A good knowledge of the above, and of knots and splices, models, sail drill, and names of the international code signal flags.

To pass from third into second class: A good knowledge of the above; also of anchor and cask, to make grummets and cringles, to point and whip a rope, loosing and furling sails, sending topgallant masts and yards up and down, and reefing topsails.

To pass from second to first class: A good knowledge of all the above, and to know how to make a reef point and gaskets; to worm, parcel, and serve a rope; to strap a block, to put on a seizing, and turn in a dead-eye.

Boys in first class: in addition to all the above, will be required to know – setting up rigging, use of palm and needle, to sew a seam, to work eyelet holes, to work cringles, making mats, rule of the road at sea, use of the long line, steering by compass and sails; sail and ship, as applied to the brigantine; sail a boat; bend and unbend sails; and some knowledge of gunnery instruction.

Boys who can pass this examination will be placed on a list of 'Fit for sea'
Gunnery and small-arm instruction were obviously popular instructions on board most ships, and the part taken by the sailors of the fleet in the Zulu campaign went a long way towards removing any prejudice against making a seaman able to handle a musket, either in the minds of seamen or officers. A ten week course on board the gunnery ships consisted of four weeks instruction on gundrill, four weeks on small arms, one week on arming boats, and one week for resume and examination. A detailed time-table of the course is given in Appendix 16.

A weekly gunnery instruction report as used on Her Majesty's Ship 'Impregnable' shows that the course was an intensive one.

weekly gunnery instruction report, _____, 187__.

Instruction	Section	Subject	No of days allowed in section	No. of boys in section	No. passed out during week	No. in section over days allowed	Instructions
First	1st	Gymnastics					
	2nd	Facings, saluting, and putting on belts					
	3rd	Squad drill without arms, but with belts on					
Second	1st	Manual exercise					
	2nd	Squad drill with arms					
	3rd	Firing exercise and company drill					
Third		Cutlass drill, cuts, points, and guards					
		Review exercise					
Fourth	1st	Handspike drill, parts of gun, etc., casting, loose, etc., manning both sides, sponging, loading, and securing					
	2nd	Pointing, shifting trucks, and the different firings in slow time, using words of command					
	3rd	General truck-gun drill in quick time and using signals					
Extra		Pistol exercise					
		Cutlass drill, stick practice					
		Swimming					
		Bugle					

Number of hours during the week at instructions ....
Number of hours during the week at general quarters ....
Number of hours during the week at battalion drill ....
) 6 pounder ....
Number of shots during the week) rifle   ....
) pistol   ....
Life-buoys examined and fit for use ....
                _____ _____, Gunner.
                _____ _____, Lieutenant.

In addition to all this a routine of exercises as laid down for the boys of the 'Formidable' shows that there was a great deal more than industrial training to be carried out.

Routine of exercises

	SUMMER	WINTER
Sail drill	Every Tuesday (summer only)	
Scrub hammocks	pm 1st Tues. in month	pm 1st Tues 2nd mth
Mend and wash clothes	Every Wednesday	Every Wednesday
Air bedding	am Every Thursday	am Every Thursday
Bath for each boy	am Tues. and pm Sat.	am Tues and pm Sat.
Wash upper deck and poop	Tues, Thurs, and Sat.	am Saturday
Wash main deck	Mon, Wed, Fri, and Sat.	pm Wed and am Sat.
Wash lower deck	Daily	Messes daily, whole deck am Sat.
Wash onlop-deck and platforms) and lower storerooms)	am Wednesday	am Wednesday
Wash boats and gear) Stations for extin. fire)	am Saturday	am Saturday
Land, for recreation, ordinarily	pm Saturday	pm Saturday
Lifeboat practice	1st Sat. in month	1st Sat. in month

Swimming exercise, during Summer, as tide and weather permit, and Monday, Tuesday, Thursday and Friday, in bath, when practicable. Band practice, under master – Daily.
The daily routine includes school from 9 to 11.55 a.m., and from 1 to 4 p.m., and night school for backward boys on Monday, Tuesday, Thursday, and Friday.

The 'Clio' by 1912, had two silver and reed Bands on board – a first and second band – as well as a bugle band. The first Band was open to engagements, and in the course of the year was generally successful in obtaining a good many. The time-table for Instrumental Music Classes on the 'Exmouth' was:

Instrumental Music Classes

Day	Morning – 9 to 12	Afternoon – 2 to 4.30	Evenings 6 – 6.45
Monday	Brass and reed band	2nd class or elementary band: violin and bugle learners of watch to practice	String Band
Tuesday	String band	2nd class or elementary band: violin and bugle learners of Catch to practice	
Wednesday	String band	General drill	
Thursday	Brass and reed band	2nd class or elementary band: violin and bugle learners of watch to practice	
Friday	Brass and reed band Bugle learners to practice	2 to 4 p.m. String Band	

Chadwick maintained that the boys of the Band, although so much of their time was taken up with music, advanced more rapidly in other things than most of the other boys; some of the best seamanship lads being amongst them. Those Band boys who finally wished to go as musicians had places found for them in regimental or naval Bands, and if not accepted by these, in any case had a good and paying profession to fall back upon.

The 'Clio' boys were also instructed in carpentry, boot making and tailoring. Three occupations not only useful for a sailor, but also for life ashore. The standard required on the 'Exmouth' in tailoring was that every boy on going aboard had to go to the tailor's shop during his watch off until he had been passed by the master tailor as fit to put a patch on, and consequently being able to repair his own clothing. Later on he was instructed in cutting out and making his own clothes.

The industrial training in boot making and tailoring was beneficial not only to the boys, but also to the institution itself. As Captain Moger reported in 1888, the 'Clio' boys had made during the year, '488 serge frocks, 562 serge trousers, 320 pairs of drawers, 238 check suits, 539 flannels, 55 canvas suits, 15 bed sackings, 133 pairs of boots, and several miscellaneous garments at a cost of £390. These if bought, would have cost at least £598. Some hundreds of garments have been repaired, as have also 350 pairs of boots and 98 bed sackings, at a cost of £29. Fifty-two thousand two hundred and twenty-one pieces of clothes have been washed at a cost of £13 for soap, etc. etc.'

It is, therefore, very little wonder that the Chief Inspector in his recommendations in 1919 stated that 'drastic reorganisation and the employment of more adult assistance to do the necessary work on the institution' would be needed in the future. So much work was being done in the Industrial Training Schools under the guise of industrial training that it had become questionable.

CHAPTER 10

Life on the 'Clio', 1879-1890

The third Annual Meeting of the supporters of the 'Clio' took place in the Town Hall, Chester, on Thursday afternoon, 26th February, 1880. Amongst the members of the committee and staff was a detachment of 120 boys from the ship, who had travelled up from Bangor by train and marched through the streets of Chester to the Town Hall headed by their band, under the command of Captain Moger and Mr Delaney, the Chief Officer. They arrived at the Town Hall at 2 p.m., and the band, 'taking up a position on the steps of the building, played a selection of lively music, whilst the remainder of the boys were drawn up in martial array in the vestibule.' On the arrival of Lord Richard Grosvenor, M.P. the Chairman for the day, the boys presented arms with 'remarkable precision'. The business meeting commenced at 3 o'clock in No. 1, Committee Room.

The committee, in presenting their Third Annual Report, were pleased to bear testimony 'to the continued prosperity of the institution.' When the committee had presented their last Report the number of boys on the 'Clio' had stood at 213. At the close of the year, 31st December, 1879, the numbers stood as follows:

Received under Sections14 and 15 Industrial Schs Act	214	Discharged	18
" " " 16 " " "	40	"	1
" " " 11 and 12 Elementary Education Act	9	"	0
" " Subscribers Nominations (£20)	9	"	1
" " " " (£10)	9	"	1
Total number received	281		

Total number discharged   23
                                        258

With 5 boys awaiting disposal this left a final total of 263.

Of these 263 boys, 92 had been received from London (7 discharged); 65 from Manchester (3 discharged); 16 from Salford; 14 from Nottingham; 7 from Blackburn; 6 from Birmingham; 3 from Widnes; 3 from Aberystwyth; 3 from Anglesey; 7 from Flint; 6 from Caernarfon; 1 from Ffestiniog; 8 from Lancashire; 1 from Rochdale; 1 from Newtown; 2 from Bootle; 2 from Oldham (1 discharged); 1 from Mold; 1 from Montgomery; 1 from Chester. The majority as we can see from the large industrial towns of England, and not as had been predicted, from Wales, Chester and the border counties.

The committee had now entered into contracts with the following authorities for the reception of boys:
School Boards: London, Liverpool, Manchester, Salford, Nottingham, Birmingham, Blackburn, Widnes, Rochdale, Wellington, Oldham, Newtown (Mont.), Bootle, Bangor, Aberystwyth, Chester (T.C.) and Mold.
Counties: Anglesey, Lancashire, Flint and Montgomery.
Board of Guardians: Ffestiniog Union.

Captain Moger, in his Report for the year, informed the meeting that of the total number of boys on board at the present time, 25 of them had neither father nor mother, 57 had no mothers, and 63 had no fathers. Of the 23 boys discharged during the year, 4 had been discharged as being physically unfit. Spalding, quoting a contemporary account described the Drury Lane Industrial School children of the same period as being 'a rickety lot, of whom any savage nation would be ashamed, and of whom an ancient Greek would probably have weeded out by some summary process of selection. They are pale, flaccid, and headachy, symptoms accompanied by sores at the angles of the mouth and nose, and at the junction of the ears with the head. Their food is well prepared but... they are dainty, wanting in appetite and sometimes even averse to food. Of the 166 children admitted within the year, 47 were below average height, 86 were below the average chest measurements. Only a minority in fact, were really healthy or perfectly formed children.'

Not only were the Industrial Schools faced with teaching or training such children, but they also had the problem of 'disposing' of them when they had been trained. Captain Moger thought it was of 'the utmost importance that an Agent should be appointed in Liverpool without delay to dispose of the boys when trained,' as there were no means of disposing of them at Bangor. Favoured forms of 'disposal' for the Industrial Training Schools included, besides joining the Army, Navy or Merchant Marine, going on the land, and emigration. Later the Colonies became more fussy, but Canada continued to take a regular supply of London's industrial school graduates. Captain Moger's concern about 'disposal' was because from 20 to 30 boys would be ready for sea during the year 1880.

The boys had made good progress in their various instruction during 1879, as Mr Henry Rogers, the Chief Inspector, testified following his inspection of the 'Clio' on the 27th May, 1879. The weather, however, had prevented the boys from deriving much benefit from open air drills. Although the health of the boys had been very good during the later half of the year, 'in the early part of the year there were several cases of frostbite, during the severe weather, as many as 50 were on the sick list at one time, and one poor little fellow lost some of his toes.' To counteract the cold that winter the boys had taken to wearing flannel drawers, which greatly added to their comfort and health.

Great improvements had been made in the ship during the year. A swimming bath, band room, boatswain's store room and a drying room had been erected. Steam had been laid on to the baths, and the floor of the bathroom deck had been concreted. A small engine had been fitted to pump out the water boat, but a lot more remained to be done, and Captain Moger hoped that the 'special fund' being raised, and stood at £900 at the time, would be sufficient to complete all the requirements. The sick bay and the drying room were too small; the provision room and the carpenter's shop were too confined, and a new fresh water tank for the upper deck was required. The new one would be differently placed to give much more room on the upper deck.

The officers, of whom there were now 13, had discharged their various duties to Captain Moger's satisfaction, and Mr Delaney, the Chief Officer had 'been indefatigable.'

The boys had been exceptionally busy during the year. The tailoring and shoemaking accounts showed good results and 'a great saving of expense had been affected.' During the year, 459 serge frocks, 458 pairs of serge trousers, 262 flannels, 534 pairs of drawers, 73 canvas suits, 103 check shirts, 70 bed sackings, 152 pairs of boots, and several miscellaneous garments had been made at a cost of £300. These things if made on shore would have cost at least £500: and some hundreds of garments had been repaired, as also had 392 pairs of boots and 800 bed sackings at a cost of £59. These if repaired on shore would have cost at least £150. 37,000 pieces of clothing had been washed at a cost of £18.

The school had made great progress under the able management of Mr Shaw and his assistants. There were now 63 boys in Standard I; 80 in Standard II; 59 in Standard III; 37 in Standard IV; and 20 in Standard V, which had been formed since the last examination in May, 1879. 43 boys had passed from Standard I to II, 40 from Standard II to III, 31 from Standard III to IV, and 20 from Standard IV to the newly formed Standard V. The Band had also made real progress since the appointment of Mr Jackson as Musical Instructor, 'and the boys now sing remarkably well.'

The additional officers appointed during the year apart from Mr Jackson, the Musical Instructor, had been a Clerk, a Seaman Instructor, and an Assistant Schoolmaster. Captain Moger believed that an additional Carpenter would be very useful, and with this exception the staff was ample for the present purposes.

At the end of the 'Clio's' third year of being in existence the 'Cheshire Observer' was quick to note that 'the boys were not all drawn from Chester and North Wales, but very far from that. Indeed, if the ship had had to rely upon that district alone, she would have been a failure. The large centres of population have come to the rescue.'

During 1880 the 'Clio's' committee had, in addition to those mentioned in their previous report, entered into contracts for the reception of boys with the School Board of Llandudno, and the County Authorities of Caernarfonshire, Denbighshire and Cheshire. 39 new boys were admitted during the year and 37 discharged. Of these 37, 29 had been sent to sea, seven had been sent home to friends, one being considered to be physically unfit, and the remaining one classed as discharged had died on board as the result of an accident. He was John Heally, who according to Dr Owen's report 'must have been, judging from the nature of the injuries received, instantly killed by a fall from the rigging.'

Captain Moger regretted in his report for 1880, that the standard of entry required of the boys to enter into Third Class Naval Reserve was prohibitory, and consequently there was no way of binding the boys to a seafaring life. After one trip they invariable went home to see their so called friends who persuaded them not to go to sea again. An application had been made by the committees of nine of the Industrial Training Ships to the Admiral Superintendent of Royal Naval Reserves, H.R.H. The Duke of Edinburgh, soliciting him to use his influence with the Lords Commissioners of the Admiralty by persuading them to reduce the standard of entry.

Ninety of the boys would be ready for the sea during 1881, and it was therefore invaluable that an Agent in Liverpool had been appointed in 1880 to ship the boys, as it was hoped that 70% of the 90 due to leave were likely to be 'shipped'.

The health of the boys with the exception of a few cases of 'mild' frostbite had been quite good. Captain Moger was still not happy about the ship's position, and asked if a sub-committee could be formed 'to enquire into the desirability of removing the ship to a more sheltered anchorage.' He considered the present site to be 'too much exposed and unsafe in bad weather.' Nine cases of measles had broken out during the year, having 'originated in a freshcomer, who brought the epidemic on board dormant within himself at the time of admission.'

As a result of the 'special fund' instigated the previous year, 'wonderful improvements' had been made in the ship during 1880. A Top Gallant Forecastle, 75 feet long had been erected. Under this had been placed the carpenter's shop, the sick ward, the tailor's shop, the new water tank and the vegetable house. The galley and provision rooms had been placed in the hold. The Band room, boatswain's and carpenter's store rooms, paint room, and shoemaker's shop had been fitted up abaft the bathroom in the after hold. The main deck had been cleared away forward, and there was now plenty of room for the boys to play in bad weather.

A lift had been fitted to carry the provisions to the lower deck from the galley. A drying room, capable of holding 700 pieces of clothes at one time, had been erected. Ports had been cut between ventilators on the lower deck, and several minor alterations had been made which had greatly 'increased the comfort of the boys'. Captain Moger, however, was not satisfied with his own quarters. He found them 'too circumscribed, and not at all comfortable in many ways.'

The tailoring and shoemaking accounts, again showed 'good

results', saving in the region of £200 on clothes and boots if they had been bought on shore. The laundry had surpassed itself during the year; some 49,296 pieces of clothes having been washed at a cost of £35.11s.6d., these if washed ashore would have cost at least £250.

The school continued to progress under Mr Shaw and his assistants. The boys now attended school by Watches instead of classes. The Vth Standard had been abolished as most of the older boys had gone to sea, and an Upper IVth Standard had been introduced instead. This was composed of the most intelligent boys who could read the Vth Standard books. Most of the boys received during 1880, 'especially the Welsh boys, were very ignorant on admission, and had to be placed in the lower Standards.'

The Assistant Chief Inspector was fairly satisfied with the conditions on the 'Clio' when he carried out his inspection of 26th May, 1880. He examined the Starboard Watch in the schoolroom and the Port Watch at their naval instructions. The education was thoroughly well attended to, and the progress made since the previous year was 'highly creditable to the teachers employed.' On the industrial training he reported that 'the nautical training and exercises are very carefully and practically attended to. Instructions were going on on the rule of the road, life-saving apparatus, signal code, sail making, canvass bag making, fender making, knotting, splicing and slining, etc.'

The 'Clio's' staff for 1880 consisted of the Captain-Superintendent, Captain W. M. Moger, R.N., Chief Officer, Mr Delaney; Schoolmaster, Mr Shaw; and two assistants, Mr Hall and Mr Davies; four naval instructors, including a gunnery instructor. A Clerk, Bandmaster, tailor, shoemaker and sick-bay attendant, two carpenters, a cook and storekeeper.

The average number of boys maintained on the 'Clio' for the year was 266, at a total cost of £6,506.5s.2d. The comparative cost per head on ordinary maintenance and management being £24.9s.2d., this being a net cost per, including profit or loss on industrial departments of £23. The industrial profits for the year were £465.4s.5d.

Of the nine boys discharged during the three years 1877-79, five were doing well, one was doubtful, one had been convicted of crime, and it was not known what had become of the other two.

In his Twenty-fourth Annual Report the Chief Inspector was concerned that 'Although the existing Reformatory and Industrial Schools Acts were drawn up with great care and have worked well up to the present time, it must be remembered that they were framed when the movement which aimed at the reformation of children through the medium of schools of detention was in its infancy, and when the children to be dealt with were composed of but two classes, the one actually criminal, the other on the road to becoming so. We have now to deal with a third and rapidly increasing class composed of children who have committed offences against the Education Acts.'

The interest shown in the question of punishment for juvenile offenders during the past year would probably have some bearing on the future of Reformatory and Industrial Schools. Lord Derby in a speech at Manchester had suggested that juvenile offenders should be punished by having 'two or three months detention in a school where the work is hard, where there is little or no play, where the life generally is rough and unattractive.' The noble Lord had obviously not visited any of the country's Reformatory and Industrial Schools, and found out that this was what was already actually happening, but for longer periods than the two or three months he suggested. However, the Chief Inspector envisaged the decline of the Industrial Training Schools and the eventual formation of Borstals with the 'development of Reformatories or of Schools of detention for short periods of somewhat similar character, under some other name.'

The Reformatories had done their work well, and since 1854 when there were 13,981 juvenile commitments, the number had decreased to 6,800 by 1881. The general character of the children committed to Reformatories had changed since the early days of the movement. The schools for young thieves and the gangs of hardened young ruffians which used to be met with in any large town had ceased to exist, and although a boy may not have been caught in a first or second offence, he seldom had time to become the hardened and desperate criminal such as might have been courted by the score before Redhill became the prioneer of Reformatories.

In 1881, there were eleven training ships, three of which were for the reception of Reformatory cases, namely the 'Akbar' and the 'Clarence' in the Mersey, and the 'Cornwall' in the Thames. There were eight Industrial School Ship's; the 'Clio', the 'Mount Edgcumbe' at Saltash, the 'Wellesley' at South Shields, the 'Shaftesbury' in the Thames, the 'Formidable' near Bristol, the 'Southampton' in the Humber, the 'Cumberland' in the Clyde, and the 'Mars' in the Tay. There was also the 'Havannah' at Cardiff, but this could scarcely be called a training ship.

The teachers in the Reformatory and Industrial Schools in spite of the disadvantage of not being recognised by the Education Department were generally painstaking and equal to their work. Although many of the School Managers believed that the difficulty in obtaining efficient teachers was because they were not being recognised by the Education Department, the Chief Inspector thought that it was because in many establishments the teacher was required 'to devote all the time not taken up in teaching to assisting in the general management of the school, in keeping order out of school, and in constant supervision even at night; and this with a rate of pay frequently less than can be obtained in Elementary Schools, where the work is over when the schoolroom is closed, and the teacher always has his evenings to himself for relaxation or study.'

On the 'Clio', Mr Rogers, the Chief Inspector, found 'three capable and experienced teachers at work in the school. They all appeared to me to be well qualified for their work. Mr Shaw, the head teacher, I have known for some years. He is a man of much experience in our work, and directs his aims to making the education given sound, real, and substantial. Mr Halle is a certified teacher. Mr Cook, an assistant , who was then doing well. All were striving hard for excellence.'

The teaching on the 'Clio' came up to the expected standards, but the Chief Inspector was quick to point out that 'it must always be clearly borne in mind that the boys in our Training Ships are half-timers only. It is unreasonable and unfair to suppose that in all respect such boys can in every point of view be brought to stand such a test as is applied in the ordinary full time Elementary Schools.'

During 1881, the 'Clio' committee entered into agreements with Congleton and Runcorn School Boards, and Merioneth County. There were 235 boys on board, and since the 'Clio' had been in existence as a school nearly 100 boys had been given a 'good start in life'. The Annual Report went on to say that '74 of these boys were following the sea as a profession, and earning good wages; one has joined the American Navy, after having been rejected by our Royal Naval Reserve, he being a quarter of an inch too short; and one has joined the Royal Navy as a warrant officer's servant.' Of the others discharged, many were in good situations on shore, and doing well.

The 'Clio's Fifth Annual Report carried a selection of letters from the boys that had left the ship. These letters were to be a regular feature of the Annual Reports, and testified to the standard of education these boys received on the 'Clio', and also to how much they actually looked upon the place as 'home', and the staff as 'friends'. A selection of these letters, which are of

119

great interest, is given in Appendix 21.

The boys' behaviour had left much to be desired during the year 1881, having 'given a great deal of trouble, and caused much anxiety.' According to the Inspector's Report, they had broken into a cabin and the provisions store. There had also been some cases of petty theft, disobedience, bad language, lying, and insolence. It prompted Captain Moger to ask 'if the parents or guardians, brothers, sisters, cousins, uncles, or aunts of these boys are not able (with all the power and love they possess) to control one child, how can we be expected to control two or three hundred if our hands are tied, as some people would wish to tie them?' The Captain maintained, however, 'that flogging is for the bad and not for the good. The fear of it is as beneficial as its use.'

One death had taken place during the year, and that was from Acute Pneumonia. One case of Scarletina had occurred, and the boy had been removed immediately to the workhouse infirmary.

The industrial training accounts showed good returns for the year, and the school had made good progress, 'not withstanding the adverse report of the Manchester School Board Examiner.'

At the close of 1881, the total number of children under sentence of detention in Reformatories and Industrial Schools was 23,693 – 19,037 boys and 4,656 girls. The Chief Inspector thought that the mixing of children sent for short terms of detention for truancy and offences against the Education Act and of those sent for a term of years was unfair and prejudicial to both cases. He believed that the former required a 'more deterrent system of treatment than is advisable in Industrial Schools. I should like to see Industrial Schools kept strictly for police cases, as was originally intended, and educational cases dealt with only in Truant Schools or Day Industrial Schools.'

The Executive Committee of the 'Clio' were concerned about their financial state at the close of the year 1882, their credit balance having been exhausted and showing a deficit of £237.15s.1d., whereas at the end of 1881 it showed a credit of £605.13s.4d. This had been because of the falling off in number of boys received on board, resulting in a loss of revenue from the Treasury and the School Boards. Extra expenditure had been necessary to keep up the Home for the boys recently established in Liverpool.

During the summer of 1882 there was a very serious outbreak of typhoid in Bangor. The 'Clio' did not escape, and nine boys went down with the fever. Two boys died during the year, one from typhoid and the other from acute meningitis.

The question of the 'Clio's' mooring position was again brought under discussion. Mr Rogers, the Chief Inspector, in his Report for the year pointed out that Captain Moger still believed 'that the position of the "Clio" is a very dangerous one, and that it cannot be retained without very serious and unnecessary risk to the lines of both officers and boys. No such risk ought to be incurred.' He himself agreed with the Captain that the position was one of great exposure and he doubted whether the physical strength of the young children sent to the 'Clio' ought to be taxed to the degree that it was during many months of the year in an unsheltered situation. As it happened, the boys had great difficulty in getting ashore to attend the Annual General Meeting at Chester on Monday, 12th February, 1883.

In a letter to Mr Rogers on behalf of the sub-committee appointed to consider the 'Clio's' position, Mr H. T. Brown, the secretary, reported that they had made an entirely unanimous report in favour of the ship remaining where she was now. 'Those who are, and have been for years, well acquainted with the Menai Strait, and whose professional opinion is entitled to at least as much weight as Captain Moger's, consider that the position of the Clio is not a dangerous one, and that serious unnecessary risk to lives of both officers and boys can only arise from carelessness or negligence.'

During the year Mr Shaw, the head schoolmaster, left the 'Clio', having been appointed to a Truant School under the Brighton School Board. Great difficulty had been encountered in replacing him, but Captain Moger had eventually secured the services of a Naval Schoolmaster who had had several years' experience in the Naval Training Ships. One of the Assistant Schoolmasters had also left to take up a shore appointment, as well as the Music Instructor, Mr Jackson. His leaving had meant that the band had to be abolished.

Although Mr Rogers's Report following his inspection on 27th May, 1882, was a favourable one and that he was well satisfied with the state of the school, 1882 as a whole had not been a happy one for the 'Clio'. Two boys had died, key members of staff had left and there had been difficulty in replacing them. The school was running at a loss, and there was by now obvious friction between the Captain-Superintendent and the Executive Committee concerning the 'Clio's' anchorage.

1883 was not to be without its problems either, although the ship was now overfull by the end of November, and all entries had to be stopped. All London School Board cases had been drafted away and the ship's outlay had exceeded the revenue by about £200. Mr Halle, the Assistant Schoolmaster, had to leave through ill health; a seaman instructor had left 'to better his position', and Mr Davison, the shoemaker and sick ward attendant had also left. There had been the usual difficulties in replacing them.

The school continued to make satisfactory progress and it had been found necessary to form a VI Standard. However, many of the boys on entry were 'very ignorant' and nearly all of them had to start in the lower Standard. One schoolmaster gave his whole time to the backward boys, who attended school daily, and by this were soon able to pass into the II Standard, when they only attended school on alternate dates.

Captain Moger thought the year 1884 opened 'more satisfactorily than any of its predecessors.' The deficit in the 'Clio's' revenue account had been reduced as a result of the Committee's appeal to the several public authorities for an increase of 6d per boy per week towards the cost of running the ship. The Committee, however, were rather apprehensive about a circular from Her Majesty's Inspector of Reformatory and Industrial Schools, which informed them that the Home Secretary, Sir William Vernon Harcourt, desired that 'no boy shall under any circumstances whatever be discharged from a Reformatory or Industrial School for sea, etc., without the full knowledge and consent of his parents.' They wished to stress that the object of the Society was for the reception and training of boys for the sea, and that if this training was merely that 'a boy shall be returned to his former evil surroundings at the end of his training, either by the design or at the caprice of worthless parents, who have in many cases by their neglect to discharge their duty done so much towards the degredation and ruin of their children, the great good at present resulting from the Institution will be seriously jeopardised, and in many cases a positive cruelty inflicted upon the boys.' Representations would be made to the authorities to induce the Home Secretary to rescind the resolution which would 'seriously endanger the continued success of every Training Ship.'

The educational standard for the year had been satisfactory, the boys' health had been good, apart from a few cases of chilblains and colds. There had been one change on the staff; Mr Slater replacing Mr Morris as Second Assistant. The ship itself, however, was only in a 'fairly good condition', and some repairs would be necessary. The ship's moorings had been examined during the summer by government divers and found to be in good order. The boys had been taken for a trip to Conway by Mr Morgan, of Garth Ferry, in the steamer 'Menai', and they had attended Fetes at Baron Hill and Mostyn Hall.

1885 was a fairly quiet year. Education and industrial training were of a high standard when the ship was inspected on the 15th May. There were no deaths and the boys looked 'healthy, strong and thriving', although some had suffered from 'pleurisy and pneumonia, and of jaundice, and a few cases of debility; one of heart disease and a few scrofulous cases.'

The 'Clio's' Tenth Annual Report shows that the boys' state of health for the following year, 1886, as being 'satisfactory'. There were a few cases of 'ordinary sickness', one case of erysipelas, one of tonsilitis, one scabies, and one case of mumps. The boys' behaviour had improved and punishments had decreased, only one boy being transferred to a Reformatory during the year. The education and industrial training was of the usual high standard, although Captain Moger had been forced to take a holiday at Royat-les-Baines, in June, due to ill health, leaving the 'Clio' in the charge of Mr Delaney. Captain Moger had been advised by his doctors to continue his visits to Royat for the next two years, advice which he found to be 'rather costly work.' The strain on the Captain must have been quite heavy. There is no mention of him having a break of any kind during the 'Clio's' first ten years of existence. Living conditions for him and his wife on board the 'Clio' must have been quite spartan. The Chairman of the Annual General Meeting at Chester in 1885, sympathised with them at the discomfort they 'were subjected to occasionally by the stormy weather in the Menai Strait, and their domestic difficulty in not being able to find servants who would consent to be pitched about on those Straits.'

During 1885, the Committee had entered into an agreement with the Dublin Protestant Orphan Society, and 17 boys had been received on board the 'Clio'. The Home in Liverpool continued to carry on its good work and it was well used by the 'Clio' old boys returning from voyages.

1886 and 1887 were again fairly uneventful years, and the

boys continued to make good progress with their studies. Their health had been good and there were no deaths, there had however, been one serious case of pneumonia, and one very severe accident, both of which thoroughly recovered. Mr Wearn, the ship's tailor died rather suddenly on the 11th July, 1887, and the shoemaker applied for this discharge about the same time.

There was still concern that the ship was carrying out its intended purpose of training boys for the sea. Of the 106 boys that left during the year, 47 were returned to their homes, and the Committee thought 'that to a great extent the expenditure on their education was a failure.'

The Committee were also concerned about the well-being of the staff. Captain Verney pointed out that at the Annual General Meeting that many of the officers in the Industrial Training Ships and Reformatories had 'started in their situations some twenty-five or thirty years ago with the first inception of the work, full of zeal for the general good. They did not stop to haggle over the terms of their income; they were stirred only by enthusiasm for their work. They were becoming old in their posts, partially blind, and partially deaf. They had given all their best years to the work; they had not thought of making any provision for their old age; and there were some of them today who were kept on at these institutions really out of charity.' Hardly the ideal type of staff to deal with the quality of boys that were being sent to the Industrial Training Ships.

Life on board the 'Clio' continued with the Inspector concerned about the 'amount of punishment for breaches of rule, disorder, disobedience, use of tobacco, petty pilfering, bad language, trickery and lying.' There were 16 cases of scarlet fever between April and September 1888, but these were dealt with in the ship's hospital, which had been fitted up for an emergency of this kind. A serious outbreak of influenza had broken out during 1889, 86 cases being recorded, with some complications of pneumonia, bronchitis and acute rheumatism.

During the same year one boy died from phthisis.

The educational state was 'carefully attended to', and in industrial training the boys were given 'careful daily instruction in the usual naval routine.' Gunnery drill, rifle and cutlass drill formed part of the course. The appliances for naval instruction were of a modern type. 'During the spring and summer months the boys go aloft, and there are yards fitted up on the main deck for winter practice. Classes of boys work with the tailor, shoemaker, and sailmaker, and a class work with the carpenters, keeping the ship in good repair. Some assist in the galley with the cook.'

The 'Clio' had become a tough penal institution, punitive and retributive in conception, and in a day when life outside the ship was bleak and savage, for the children who found their way inside, the regime had to be correspondingly severe if it was to be regarded as a deterrent.

CHAPTER 11

Problems with the code of 1895, and the difficulty of obtaining boys

The last decade of the nineteenth century was heralded by a wave of educational enthusiasm in Wales with the passing of the Welsh Intermediate Education Act in 1899. There followed the establishment of the Scheme for Caernarfonshire in 1893, and by 1897 there were eleven Secondary or County Schools established throughout the country.

The Local Taxation (Custom and Excise) Act of 1890 alloted the 'whisky money' to the county and county borough councils, money which could be devoted to the provision and improvement of secondary and technical education. This tendency to favour the county and municipal authorities rather than the School Boards showed that the government was beginning to realise that the School Boards, especially in rural areas were not as successful as they had hoped they would be. The 'payment by results' system disappeared. The reorganisation of the central authority was made possible by the Board of Education Act, 1899, which co-ordinated the various activities of Whitehall and South Kensington, and replaced the Committee of Council and the Science and Art Department by a Central Board of Education with greatly extended powers.

The Royal Commission on the Housing of the Working Classes, appointed in 1884, resulted in the Housing Act of 1890. Authorities were encouraged to adopt improvement schemes such as Birmingham's, and their powers to demolish single insanitary houses and to engage in house building were strengthened. Charles Booth in his survey of 'The Life and Labour of the People of London' saw that 'popular education has been far from wasted even in the case of those who may seem to have learnt but very little. Obedience to discipline and rules of proper behaviour have been inculcated; habits of order and cleanliness have been acquired; and from these habits self-respect arises.' The working man was to have his own Parliamentary Labour Party by the beginning of the twentieth century. People of the calibre of Lloyd George, as he put it himself, were being 'carried forward on a tide of social pity that was only waiting for a chance of expression.'

The Inspector found the 'Clio' on the day of his inspection, 24th March, 1891, still maintaining her 'high character for practical and complete efficiency, and for careful management.' On the day of inspection there were 262 boys on board. Of these, 250 were under legal detention, the remainder were on the voluntary list. The boys had a bright and healthy appearance, and looked clean and well cared for, and although they were small in stature, they were active and sprightly.

From the health point of view the year had been a favourable one. 'A few cases of pneumonia, with some cases of delicacy from the influenza attack of 1890. Some cases of mumps, a few strumous cases, and some cases of jaundice. Some eye disorders of the usual kind, one case of hernia, and a few ordinary wounds and bruises.'

Education and industrial training was of the usual high standard. There had been some trouble during the year with a group of boys of 'bad character', and one boy had 'worked much mischief' which resulted in him being transferred to a Reformatory. There had been an attempt to set fire to the carpenter's shop, two cases of absconding, and the usual use of bad language, bullying, and smoking. However, 'the general aspect, in spite of all difficulties, was hopeful and satisfactory.'

There was an attack of influenza in June, 1891, and 41 cases of the same epidemic in January and February, 1892. During the year there had been a few severe colds and inflamed eyes; one severe case of pneumonia; three cases of jaundice; some cases of rheumatism and some sore throats; one case of pneumonia with effusion; one death from typhoid and pneumonia. The boys' behaviour had not improved, there being several cases of 'theft, insolence, disobedience, disorder, insubordination, fighting and striking, use of bad language, filthy habits, lying and use of tobacco.' However, the Inspector was happy to report that 'the boys were under careful and regular school instruction.'

The Inspector's Report for 1893, and 1894, are very brief, there being nothing new to report. The educational state of the ship being 'well attended to', the industrial training being given under 'careful instruction.' There were the continual cases of eczema, bad eyes, sprained ankles, enlarged glands, one fracture from a fall, one case of jaundice, a few influenza cases of a mild type, and one case of pneumonia.' The boys were still disobedient, using bad language, insubordinate, quarrelsome, bullying each year, and there had been one serious attack upon another boy. Despite all this, the boys were in 'good spirits and well affected', and the Inspector was happy that the order and discipline on the 'Clio' was being 'well maintained'.

With the publication of the Education Department's new Code in 1895, the Chief Inspector wanted it 'clearly understood' that in the Reformatory and Industrial Schools they were 'really working up in elementary and class subjects to the standard of ordinary elementary schools.' The question of industrial training, particularly of boys, and the proper division between such training and ordinary schooling was one of considerable difficulty. He wished to point out that the boys' schools, both Reformatory and Industrial, were divided into various classes. 'There are the ships, where of course the industrial labour is mainly such as will fit the boys for a sea life; there are the farm or country schools, where the work is mainly farming and market gardening; there are the suburban schools, many of which have a fair-sized market garden attached, and there are the town schools where instruction is given in various trades, prominent among which are shoemaking, and tailoring. In a good many schools woodchopping is carried on and this, where done by hand, must be regarded as perhaps the lowest form of occupation which can be said to have any qualities for industrial training. But it is to be borne in mind that to get through a normal day a certain amount of occupation, whatever its worth intrinsically, is necessary, and that an important part of the value of the training in a Reformatory or Industrial School lies in the inculcation of habits of industry, in addition to what is done towards the teaching of a trade.'

In March, 1895, a Government inquiry was carried out into the dismissal of Captain Statham from the command of the 'Clarence' following on out-break of small pox on board the ship in November, 1894. The ensuing row resulted in the Secretary of State withdrawing the 'Clarence's' certificate as from 30th November, 1895. A special inquiry was carried out into the condition of the Industrial School Ship 'Wellesley' following a number of complaints having been made to the Home Office.

Captain Moger was not without his worries either. Mr Delaney, the First Officer, had retired through ill health. The number of boys on board the 'Clio' was the lowest for 16 years. There were 34 vacancies, 60 boys were to be discharged during the year, and there were very few voluntary cases. The Captain-Superintendent believed that the falling off in numbers had been mainly due to the fact that since the establishment of the 'Clio' many new and philanthropic societies had come into being. Since the number of boys on board the 'Clio' had fallen so low, and if the numbers were not maintained, there would be the question of reducing the number of staff. Captain Moger suggested that 'there were plenty of Roman Catholic boys, who, no doubt, would come into the ship subject to the leave of the Roman Catholic authorities.' The Committee were not fully in agreement with him, although they thought it 'far better that the Roman Catholic boys should be saved from going to wrack and ruin even under Protestant supervision.' Anyway, they thought 'the Roman Catholic priest at Bangor had as much as he could do in his district without embarking upon the work the 'Clio' would give him.' Despite this feeling of antagonism towards the Roman Catholic Church the Committee agreed in the end to communicate with them 'with a view of ascertaining whether it would be possible to take any Roman Catholic boys in the ship.'

During 1896, the questions surrounding the purposes of the Reformatory and Industrial Training Ships still raised their heads. The Inspector in his report for the year 1896 stressed that the primary objects of these ships was not to make sailors out of the boys. 'The primary object of the ships, as of the shore schools, whether farm schools or town schools, was to endeavour to make decent citizens, obtaining an honest livelihood, of children who had actually committed crime or whose disposition or home surroundings were such as to cause them to be in danger of taking to criminal courses later on in life.'

The Inspector, in the same report, still complaints that the boys were not getting enough exercise ashore, although they went occasionally to the public ground at Gallows Point, which was, however, 'too far off (1½ miles) to be of much use.' All the boys were taken to 'Llandudno or some other seaside resort for a day's trip each summer.' The hurricane deck served as an open air playground for the boys, and although there was a swimming bath installed in the hold, this could not be used during the winter months. There was a good library of books on board. The boys set up 'an entertainment amongst themselves', and were given an occasional 'lantern' show during the winter by Captain Moger.

The doctor visited the ship twice a week and oftener when necessary. Each boy was examined by the doctor, in the presence of the captain, every 3 months. 'The boys on admission are mostly undersized and sometimes too sickly for sea life. The hopeless cases are weeded out by the doctor at the quarterly inspections, and the others, though generally small, are by means of daily baths and fresh air made healthy and smart.'

As an alternative to the various punishments a mark system had been introduced on the 'Clio' with rewards from 2d to 1s a month for 60 boys. Quarterly prizes were given in the schoolroom and extra rewards for good work in the tailor's shop. By 1897, the Inspector was pleased to report that 'the mark system and quarterly prizes seem to do their work well in keeping the boys up to the mark.' No cell case had been reported during the year. The boys' behaviour during the following year was not so good. There were 19 boys found smoking, 10 stealing (mostly food from the galley), 4 were punished for fighting and 9 for bullying. A further 4 were punished for 'dirty conduct', 4 for indecency, one for indecent language, 2 for tampering with lamps, one for insolence, and eight for misconduct in school or during punishment. 'Ten of the above cases were punished by confinement in cells, the rest by birch.' The cells were to be used again on four occasions during 1899.

The year 1899, also saw Captain Moger suffering from ill health. Concern was shown at the Annual General Meeting about the number of boys on the ship from North Wales and Cheshire. Compared to the 250 boys received from Lancashire during the year, only 43 had been received from Cheshire, and 17 from Flintshire and the surrounding district.

Messrs Elder Dempster and Co., the well known shipping form of Liverpool, had written to Captain Moger in March, 1899, stating that they had decided to carry two boys from the 'Clio' on their steamers. They also required another two for their coast steamers, and would be calling on Captain Moger to supply them with boys from time to time in the future. They were willing to pay the boys a wage of 10s per month during the first year, £1 the second year, and £2 for the third year.

By the end of 1899, Captain Moger was forced through ill health to resign from his post as Captain-Superintendent of the 'Clio'. The Inspector, in his Report for 1900, gave him the following testimonial: 'The year has been marked by the resignation of Captain Moger, who commanded this ship from the very first, and to whose skill and ingenuity are due many of the features on board which leave the 'Clio' a model. The loss is a severe one, but it is gratifying to find under fresh auspices promise of a new lease of vigorous life.'

CHAPTER 12

A new century, a new captain

Commander Frederick G. C. Langdon, R.N., was appointed as the new Captain-Superintendent of the 'Clio' in December, 1899. There were 24 applicants for the post of Captain-Superintendent, and out of the five selected by a sub-committee to be submitted to the General Committee 'the appointment was given by an almost unanimous vote to Commander Langdon of London.' He was obviously a man of experience, having entered the Royal Navy in December, 1865. On leaving the Service he had taken up a position on the Industrial Training Ship 'Black Prince', a position he held for three years.

The first year of the new Captain-Superintendent's term of office was a quiet one, although his first month on board the 'Clio' must have been rather a bleak one, the weather in January, 1900, being bad enough for the Bishop of Bangor to confirm 70 of the 'Clio' boys on board the ship rather than in the Cathedral. The Society suffered a great loss by the death of its President, the Duke of Westminster. Several expensive repairs to the 'Clio' had to be carried out during the year; the most expensive being the lifting and relaying of the ship's moorings at a cost of £260. On his visit the Inspector had found the educational standard on board to be 'good'; the nautical training 'as described in previous reports'; the boys' behaviour satisfactory; and their health 'good'.

The 'Clio's' Medical Officer agreed that the general health of the boys had been good, although several of them had suffered from high temperatures lasting for a few days, 'and generally associated with derangements of the stomach'. His main concern was that 'many of the boys have also suffered from inflammation of the Burse near the knee-joint, and even in some cases spreading to the knee-joint itself; all caused by 'kneeling' in washing decks. As these cases have been so frequent ever since my connection with the ship, I should be glad if the 'kneeling' could be done away with altogether.' The ship's doctor at least was concerned about what was considered to be industrial training, but was in effect child labour.

Mr Legge, the Chief Inspector, was not of the same opinion. Dr Lloyd's letter had been forwarded to the Secretary of State's office by mistake, and since it was one of the ship's quarterly reports, it should, in fact, have been forwarded direct to Mr Legge's office. In a memorandum to the Secretary of State he argued that the danger of the complaint commonly called housemaid's knee 'can be obviated to a large extent, but it is, I believe, quite common for sailors to kneel down when scrubbing decks, and the boys will have to become inured to it.' Scrubbing decks on their knees was, therefore, according to Mr Legge, part of the boys' industrial training.

It is incredible to think that some of the boys admitted on board the 'Clio' were ever considered as suitable for a seafaring life. Although the authorities were bound to fill in a fairly stringent medical report, considering the exposed position of the ship, and the daily routine the boys were expected to follow, it is little wonder that the 'Clio's' annual medical reports were as long as they were. Practically every report complains of the boys' small stature, and of many with 'marked tuberculous tendencies.' One boy admitted during 1902 'had broken his arm before admission and it was found necessary to amputate the limb.' However, many boys were refused admission to the 'Clio' as 'never likely to make good sailors', and places were found for them in shore schools.

The year 1901, was again a fairly quiet year on board the 'Clio'. A new platform had been fitted up on the ship's side for the purpose of 'heaving the lead.' An additional playing field on shore had been rented. The brass band had been reformed, and the Admiralty had lent the ship a seven-pounder field gun, at the request of Captain Langdon, and 'the boys were quickly learnt the drill which was both useful and showy.'

The year was not without its problems though, and following the dismissal from an Admiralty Training Ship of an ex– 'Clio' boy, the question of the number of boys from the Industrial Training Ships finally deciding on making the sea a career, especially the Royal Navy, again reared its head. Lengthy correspondence followed the discharge of one Arthur Byron from HMS 'Lion'.

Arthur Byron had been committed to the 'Clio' in April 1898, by the Nottingham School Board for truanting. 'During his stay in the School Ship he developed into a strong, intelligent and reliable lad; and at the age of 16 was drafted to one of the Admiralty Training Ships, with an excellent character from his school.' The Admiralty Training Ships Authorities themselves found him to be of 'an exemplary character, clean in his dress and person, and gave promise of making a strong, useful seaman.' Unfortunately, the Admiralty discovered that Byron, some years before his committal to the 'Clio', had been charged for, but not convicted of, 'two cases of childish theft.' Consequently, it was directed that he should be discharged from the Navy, 'apparently in accordance with an utterly mechanical and most cruel interpretation of an Admiralty rule that no boy who has been either committed for, or charged with, any criminal offence, can be admitted into HM Ships.'

The Nottingham School Board desired 'to urge most strongly that the Admiralty rule in question should not be so mechanically and rigorously interpreted as to deprive deserving boys, such as the one under consideration, of an opportunity of joining the Navy, and the country at large of the service of most promising additions to His Majesty's Navy, in cases, where in the face of most excellent testimonials as to character and fitness extending over a series of years, some childish peccadilloes have been discovered.'

In a further letter on behalf of the Nottingham School Board, Mr Abel, informed Captain Langdon that the By-laws committee had decided to bring the case before the House, 'but that neither the name of the boy nor of the ship shall be mentioned.' The question had been put down by Mr Bond, M.P., but was not eventually put before the House. Mr Legge reported to the Secretary of State that Captain Langdon had asked to 'have the name of the ship and the boy kept quiet, for fear, I suppose, of reprisals.'

The Inspector believed that it was cases like Byron's that explained why the Army was so much more popular than the Navy, even with boys on the Industrial School Ships. The 'Shaftesbury', for instance, sent in the years 1897 to 1899, 46 boys into the Navy, but 86 into the Army. Another of the Training Ships, the 'Mars', had a case similar to Byron's that occurred there a few years previously, 'with the result that in the code of honour, which obtains even among Industrial School Boys, it is considered bad form on the 'Mars' to volunteer for the Navy.'

On taking up the matter of admitting boys convicted of theft in the Navy, with the Admiralty, the Secretary of State was informed that the view they took was that as they could get a sufficient supply of boys who had not been convicted of theft, it seemed rather unfair to take on boys who had been convicted. There was also the problem of the convicted boy introduced into a ship being resented by the other seamen, and that there was a 'tendency to put down all lost articles to his account.' There was exactly the same problem of getting boys or girls from Reformatories into service in good houses where servants of good character were kept. Again, the Secretary of State had, at the request of Mr Legge, tried to get Reformatory boys into the Royal Engineers. Their answer had been, 'Why should we take boys who have been criminals, at your request, when our lists are crowded with applications from the sons of respectable sergeants in the army?'

The problem was that boys of bad character could hardly 'expect to be clothed, taught a trade at the public's expense, and then by Home Office influence put into careers that would only with difficulty be open to them if they had been honest.' However, on the other hand, where a boy criminal was 'really-reformed, there should be some means of whitewashing him, – which does not exist at present.' The Secretary of State felt that it was a problem 'so full of difficulty that it must, apparently, be left to time to deal with.'

It took until May, 1902, to finally resolve the Byron affair, when 'after further discussions and a promise from the Admiralty that their rule should not at the most extend beyond actual convictions. The Secretary of State decided to let this matter drop.'

The question of the disposal of boys, especially to sea, was however not allowed to be dropped. The Byron affair had caused the Secretary of State to look closer at the 'Clio's' returns of inmates who left on Discharge of Licence. It appeared that there was 'certainly a tendency on some of these ships to merely send home at the end of their term boys who are unfit to unwilling to go to sea. It was very obvious, as we have seen, that the type of boys sent to the Training Ships were not physically suited for a life at sea. The Secretary of State was of the opinion that many of these boys would have been better placed in a land school. He thought that it was 'a pity a proper system of exchange between land and ship schools cannot be arranged; but of course it is difficult to persuade landlords to give up well-grown boys in exchange for weaklings.'

The Secretary of State was not in the least but happy about the answer to his letter criticising the 'Clio's' disposal methods. In the absence of Captain Langdon, who was on leave, Mr Milliard, the Clerk, had replied that 'in the case of all boys who decide to go home and not to sea, the parents state that they have employment for the boy before he is discharged, if the boy decides to go to sea and his parents wish him not to, the register is consulted as to his antecedents, and in almost every case the boys goes to sea.'

It was left to Mr Legge to explain fully to the Secretary of State the position at the time. In a lengthy report he stated: 'The energies of the Department have been principally, I admit, directed towards reducing so far as possible the residue of those who are not got [*sic*] to try a sea life. There must always be such a residue, and that of this residue a fair proportion should return to friends is also inevitable, even though I impress on the schools the view that they ought to licence children even against their will if they seek to return to undesirable friends, an interpretation of the Law of which I understand the Department to by shy. A further point for consideration is that returning to good friends is probably the best means of disposal of all, and the proportion of good friends in connection with the ships is probably greater than in the ordinary shore schools, for the simple reason that as many merely Education Act cases are committed to the ships and practically no Section 15 (Larceny) cases, with the view to smoothing entry into the Navy if the boy proves fit. About one-third of the 'Clio' boys are Education Act cases. Granted all this, there is of course a residue of boys from the ships who do not go to sea and who do not return to good friends. It is with a view to them that we have taken special pains to secure that the school work on board ship is up to the best standard found on shore. On this we have been firm in spite of phrases such as 'the object is to make sailors not scholars', etc., etc., and we have got universally introduced on the

Industrial School Ships and maintained at a high level, drawing, the very basis of industrial training. We further endeavour to get the tailor's shops, the shoemaker's shops, however limited their resources, properly utilised for training, and also the ship's carpenter's shop.'

Whilst the arguments concerning the methods of disposal continued the general aspect on board the 'Clio', according to the Inspector, was 'bright and cheerful, even on a wet day, and the boys are evidently under good influence.' Four boys died during 1902. One from tubercular meningitis, one from rheumatic fever, one from pleuro-pneumonia, and one from 'suddenly choking while eating.' The boys' conduct had generally been good, apart from four cases of 'breaking out of ship' and a few cases of stealing food.'

Mr Legge, the Chief Inspector, was very satisfied with the state of the ship in 1903. The training was 'admirably adapted to fit boys for a naval life, and three features may be mentioned: 1) the fitting up and stowing away of the schoolroom desks; 2) the beautiful condition in which the mess traps are kept; 3) the attention given to style in boat pulling.'

Not all they boys, despite the attention given to boat pulling, were at ease in a boat. In the early part of 1903, Captain Langdon had to jump into the Straits to save the life of one boy that had fallen overboard, an action that resulted in the Captain receiving a letter from the Home Office stating that 'The Secretary of State has heard with great pleasure of your prompt action in jumping overboard and swimming to the rescue of the boy who had fallen out of a gig belonging to the "Clio" and was being carried away by the tide. But for your presence of mind, the boy, who it appears could not swim, would probably have drowned.'

The boys were again taken to a 'holiday encampment', following the success of the one the previous year. This new idea of having a summer camp, was not only good for the boys,

140

but had the 'additional advantage of giving the ship a beneficial rest.' A detatchment of boys spent a day in Wolverhampton 'drilling' in aid of the town's Saturday Lifeboat Fund. Baden-Powell had been given the Freedom of the Borough of Bangor in August, had visited the ship, and given the boys a 'stirring speech.'

A visit on board the 'Clio' was obviously one of the highlights for any dignitaries visiting the Bangor area, as the ship's Visitors' Book testifies. The ship was also open to the public in general. An 'Almanack Supplement' to the *North Wales Chronicle* carries the following advertisement under the 'Directory' for Bangor: The 'Clio'. Capt-Sup. Commander Langdon, R.N. Chief Officer; Mr Bromley, Clerk; Mr William Wells, Head Schoolmaster, Mr William S. Milliard. There are upwards of 250 boys on board. Open to visitors daily. Admission 1s.

It was an obvious way of getting additional revenue for the funds whilst serving to show the public that they had nothing to hide on board the 'Clio'.

The Annual General Meeting held at Chester in February, 1904, was informed that the ship had shown a slight profit for the previous year. The record of offences during the year was not a serious one apart from 'seven boys breaking into the Bandroom and damaging the instruments.' The boys were now taken twice a week, weather permitting, 'to Beaumaris Green for football or other field sports.' Although there had been four slight cases of Scarlet Fever and two cases of epilepsy, the boys' health had been quite good.

The Liverpool Home had, unfortunately, not been working 'as satisfactorily as formerly' and by 1905, it had been decided that since the officer in charge had resigned his position it was time to test another mode of 'shipping' boys at Liverpool. It was proposed to engage a Mr Maurice Voss, who shipped boys on behalf of other Industrial Training Ships, as Agent for the 'Clio' boys. The Home in St George's Square would be closed down and the boys would from now on be lodged in the Sailor's Home, 'the authorities having made special arrangements for their reception.'

As if in answer to the Home Office's complaint about the disposal of boys to sea, the 'Clio's' General Committee in their 28th Annual Report quoted that since the existence of the 'Clio', no fewer than 2,018 boys had received training on board the ship, the majority of whom had passed into the Royal Navy and the Mercantile Marine, and some into the Army. The figures for the last three years showed that eleven boys had joined the Royal Navy, thirteen the Army, and 101 the Mercantile Marine. Of the boys disposed of during 1904, 81% had gone to sea. They were doing their best to fulfill the Secretary of State's wishes of having more boys sent to sea.

CHAPTER 13

Tragedy Strikes

The Times called it the 'Training Ship Tragedy.' *The Manchester Guardian* was more explicit, calling it 'Bullying on the Clio', and the *North Wales Chronicle* simply stated 'Sad Death of a Clio Boy Alleged to be due to Bullying.'

A very shaken Captain Langdon explained in a letter to Mr Legge, the Chief Inspector, the events that had lead to the 'Clio's' name being heralded in newspapers throughout the country. The letter, dated 9th February, 1906, stated:

'A most unfortunate thing had happened. A lad named Crook died this morning in the Infirmary from concussion and an inquest is ordered for tomorrow afternoon. The circumstances are these.

On Monday he was ashore at the Recreation Ground with the other boys when he complained to Mr Robinson (1st Assistant Schoolmaster) that he felt faint and couldn't walk. Mr Robinson at once had him taken on board and Mr Booth put him to bed in the sick bay. When on examining him he found some bruises on his legs Mr Booth came to tell me and I went forward and asked the boy how he got the bruises. He said, 'Oh Sir, George Singleton and J. Meredith knocked me down and kicked me yesterday (Sunday) on the Upper Deck'. This was confirmed by a little boy named Norton who came forward and gave evidence against one of them (Singleton) and both Singleton and Meredith owned up when I accused them. I had both birched for bullying, but never imagined that poor Crook was seriously injured nor did Dr Lloyd when he saw him.

On Wednesday night at 10 p.m. Mr Booth came to tell me that there appeared to be something wrong with Crook and on going to him I found him in a dazed condition and very cold in spite of the pile of blankets and hot bottles. I at once sent for Dr Lloyd who pronounced it a case of either epilepsy or concussion and on hearing my account of what had occurred he thought it must be concussion.

He injected some digitalis arsenic and c, and we got him to take a little brandy and the next morning sent him to the Infirmary, where he succumbed to his injuries this morning. Of course, this means an inquest, and is most prejudicial to the ship. The poor lad who comes from Bury has an Aunt and two sisters to whom I have twice written to inform them of the case and to ask them if any of them would attend the funeral. The boy was not very bright and so these little ruffians made a butt of him, I understand.

I have given all the boys a severe talking to on the subject of bullying and I hope it may have a good effect – they are all thoroughly frightened at present and the ship is very silent. I am sorry to say that they've been more troublesome since Mr Robertson's visit then ever before in my experience and I have felt for some time as if something were going to happen but I never thought it would be as bad as this.

I will send you a report tomorrow with the result of the inquest.'

The inquest, by Mr J. Pentir Williams, the North Caernarfonshire Coroner, and a jury, into the circumstances attending the death of William Crook, aged 13, was held at the Magistrates Room, Bangor, on Saturday, 10th February, 1906. The coroner informed the jury that the deceased had entered the 'Clio' in October, 1905. On Sunday, 4th February, 1906, it had been alleged that someone had struck the boy, 'but no importance was then attached to the incident.' On Monday, 5th, when the boys were taken to the Recreation Ground, Beaumaris, the boy had complained to the attending Schoolmaster of feeling unwell, and was returned to the ship 'with a boy being held off to assist him aboard,' and put to bed in the sick bay. According to the *North Wales Chronicle* 'Dr Lloyd was called in to see him,' but according to the Guardian and Times the doctor 'paid his ordinary visit to the 'Clio' on Monday afternoon and had his attention drawn to the case.' In his evidence Dr Lloyd simply said that he 'called at the 'Clio' on Monday afternoon.'

After seeing the boy, Dr Lloyd ordered him to be kept quiet in bed. There did not seem to be very much the matter with him, except that there were some bruises on his body, but he was able to reply to some questions, put to him quite rationally.' The bruises the doctor had mentioned were on Crook's thigh, right arm and right knee. Asked if he had questioned the boy as to how he came by his bruises the doctor answered according to the *North Wales Chronicle*: 'Yes, but I could not make much out of him. He seemed shy.' What the Chronicle omits to state is that the doctor did not ask the boy this question until the Tuesday night, when he had 'a message about nine o'clock that the boy was worse, and went aboard the 'Clio' about ten o'clock.' It was during this visit that the doctor diagnosed concussion and ordered appropriate treatment, which according to Captain Langdon's letter, was an injection of digitalis arsenic and c, and a little brandy. The doctor also suggested that Crook should be transferred to the Caernarfonshire and Anglesey Infirmary. This was not done until the following day (Wednesday), 'and Crook became unconscious on the way.' Dr Lloyd saw him several times during the Thursday and 'he got gradually worse till he become quite unconscious on Thursday night, and died about 12.30 on Friday morning (midnight).'

On the Saturday morning Dr Lloyd and Dr Middlewick, the house surgeon at the Infirmary, carried out a post-mortem. They 'found a bruise the size of a half-crown piece, under which there was considerable extravasation of blood right through the skull to the bone.' To produce such a bruise considerable violence must have been used, whether as the result of a blow or fall, and the two doctors were of the opinion 'that this was the bruise which had caused the concussion of the brain, from which they boy died.' Asked how the bruise could have been brought about in his opinion Dr Lloyd replied, 'It must have been caused by a blow, a kick or a fall, and then coming into contact with a hard substance. There was no sign of disease in the boy, all the organs being perfectly healthy. My opinion is that death was brought about by violence in some shape or form.' It seems rather incredible that no one noticed a bruise the size of a half-crown on the boy's forehead, and that boy diagnosed as having concussion, and being examined by a doctor daily from Monday, 5th, until the bruise was discovered on Saturday, 10th February.

Mr Thornton Jones, the Solicitor representing Captain Langdon and the Committee of the 'Clio', questioned Dr Lloyd at some length, and 'elicited the fact that the boy was promptly attended to by the officers the moment he reported himself unwell, and that no time was lost in securing for him such attention as he required.'

Captain Langdon was then asked to testify, and gave his version of the events leading up to Crook's death. He told the jury that he was first informed that something was wrong on the previous Monday, when the Chief Officer asked him to see Crook. He found bruises on the boy's body and asked him how he came by them. Crook informed him that two boys had knocked him down and kicked him. Asked who they were, Crook had named George Singleton and J. W. Meredith. Singleton had been on board the 'Clio' for three years, since he was ten years old, having been transferred from the Leigh Union. Both boys were on a bad character; Singleton was a bully and full of mischief, Meredith was 'a perfect little demon', and

Captain Langdon was not at all surprised at him behaving in this way.

Captain Langdon had asked the Chief Officer to make enquiries, and a boy named Norton had come forward and said that he had seen Crook knocked down by Singleton. When Crook stood up he was again knocked down by him. The two boys were brought before the Captain and did not deny having bullied Crook. He ordered them both to receive twelve strokes of the birch each for bullying.

On the Tuesday night the Chief Officer came to inform Captain Langdon that Crook had taken a turn for the worse, and that he was concerned about the boy's condition. The Captain and his wife went at once to see him and decided to send for Dr Lloyd. When the doctor arrived he 'injected something into the boy's arm, which revived him.' Crook, however, appeared dazed, and moved his head from side to side, and could not reply to questions put to him. They managed to get him to take some brandy, after which he slept until the morning, when Captain Langdon and his wife paid him another visit. He was then removed to the Infirmary, at Dr Lloyd's orders, where the Captain and his wife paid him a visit on the Thursday to see how he was getting on, but they were not allowed to see him.

On finding that there was to be an inquest Captain Langdon had called in a Bangor Solicitor, Mr Thornton Jones. He verified at the inquest that 'everything that could have been done for the deceased had been done and at once.' Mr Thornton Jones, acting on Captain Langdon's instructions, had on the Saturday morning of the inquest visited the 'Clio' when the boys were paraded, and all who knew anything about the affair were ordered to stand out. About a dozen of the boys had done so, and Mr Thornton Jones had the proofs of their evidence, which he proposed to submit to the Coroner. Unfortunately all the boys' statements varied from one another.

Evidence having been given by Samuel Robinson,

Schoolmaster, and William George Booth, Chief Officer, bearing on the deceased's complaints and illness, Mr Booth said that Norton told him that he had seen Singleton abusing Crook, whereupon Singleton had been taken to the sick bay and identified by Crook as one of his assailants, and Crook had added that the other assailant was Meredith.

Mr Thornton Jones said his enquiries had resulted in the boy witnesses giving varying accounts of the incident, no doubt due to their having witnessed it at different stages of its development. The boys had mentioned that boys named Francis, Manley, and Hales had taken part in the bullying of Crook, as well as Singleton and Meredith.

The Coroner called for Christopher Norton, and according to the *Times* correspondent, 'a sturdy thirteen year old boy' went into the witness box. Norton said in evidence that the previous Sunday morning he had seen Singleton knocking Crook about. Every time Crook stood up Singleton knocked him down by jabbing him in the chest with both fists. There were a lot of boys around at the time, but no one interfered with Singleton, who kept pushing Crook to the floor. Crook fell on his back when knocked down. Meredith was not there at the time. Asked by the Coroner why Singleton did it, the witness replied that it was 'because Crook couldn't stick up for him self, sir.'

Albert Slingsby, another 'Clio' boy, aged fifteen, also gave evidence incriminating other boys. He maintained that he saw Manley hit Crook on the head with a broom handle. Manley on the other hand stated that he saw Francis kick Crook in the mouth, although Francis did not have his boots on at the time. Francis informed the Coroner that Manley had thrown Crook on the floor, and blood had come out of his mouth. When Crook stood up again Manley had hit him with a stick and he again fell to the floor. Francis and another boy had then taken Crook to Mr Staden, the Second Officer, to report the incident. The officer told them to take the boy away, and as they came out of the officer's Mess 'Meredith struck Crook a blow on the side of the head, dashing it against the bulkhead.' Francis asked Crook if he should take him to another officer, but Crook said no, he would go and clean his boots.

Before calling any more of the boys, the Coroner said it seemed to him the evidence given by the boys was rather cloudy and very contradictory, and it was quite clear that no one realised the serious nature of the injury that had been inflicted on Crook at the time – not even Dr Lloyd at first. However, it was quite clear that there had been some horse-play on the ship, and they had ample evidence as to what was the cause of death. The ship's officers and the police had mentioned Singleton and Meredith as being the main suspects, whilst as the result of Mr Thornton Jones's investigations it was quite clear that Manley was also implicated. The whole thing, however, seemed so hazy that it appeared quite impossible to saddle anyone with the responsibility for Crook's death.

Captain Langdon was recalled and asked to what extent, if any, the boys on board the 'Clio' were allowed to fight. The Captain replied that they were not allowed to fight at all.

The Coroner then asked the jury if they wished to hear the evidence of the other boys, to which they replied in the negative. Mr Pentir Williams, the Coroner, proceeded to sum up the evidence.

He said it was a duty to the public to sift the matter to the bottom, as boys were sent to the 'Clio' from all parts of the country. As to the cause of death, all the symptoms pointed to concussion of the brain. The deceased boy had inculpated the two boys, Singleton and Meredith, who, apparently, in the presence of the deceased, had admitted their share in the matter in the presence of Captain Langdon and the Chief Officer. Singleton and Meredith were both under fourteen year of age. He reminded the jury that if a man attacked another, and as the result of that attack, or as a result of any unlawful act, death ensued, it would be a case of manslaughter, or, if with intent, of murder. However, with regard to persons under the age of seven they were deemed to be absolutely incapable of any crime, and the presumption was that persons between the age of seven and fourteen were also incapable of any crime unless there was extreme viciousness or special circumstances affecting the case. The present case struck him as being a bit of rough horseplay among boys; nothing more than a squabble, and since boys would be boys, as they knew, having been boys themselves. For himself he did not think for a moment that any of the boys involved dreamt of bringing about a result such as had occurred in this case. They had been punished, and he hoped this case would be a warning to them not to repeat such conduct. What had been said about other boys was very shadowy indeed. It was for the jury to decide whether it would be necessary to take more serious notice of their conduct than had already been taken. If the jury thought, as he did, that death was the result of rough horseplay by the boys, they would return a verdict of death by misadventure. If, however, they thought the boys' act was illegal, then they would return a verdict of manslaughter. It would then be for them, the jury, to consider whether there was any reasonable prospect of any petty jury convicting on the evidence they had heard.

The jury retired to consider their verdict. It took them fifteen minutes to return a verdict of death by misadventure.

The burial of William Crook, aged thirteen, took place on Monday, 12th February, 1906, at Llandegfan Churchyard. His brother Joseph, two sisters Harriet and Eliza, were present as well as an aunt with whom William had been living prior to his being sent to the 'Clio'. He shares a grave with eleven other 'Clio' boys all aged between twelve and thirteen.

The affair was not to end there. The *North Wales Chronicle* of 16th February, 1906, reprints a letter written to the *Manchester Guardian* by Minor Canon Morrice, Chaplain to the 'Clio', in which he stated: 'In your leaderette of your issue of February 12th under the heading "The Noble Work of the Institution", I am glad to find that you state that a "second review of the facts may produce a certain measure of sympathy with Captain Langdon, who has some intractable characters to deal with, and who appears in this case to have done all that it was possible to do to help the injured boy and to punish his assailants". I venture to suggest, sir, that still closer contact with this case and the material with which Captain Langdon and his officers have to deal, and a consideration of the extraordinary immunity from misadventure of this kind, together with the creditable record of scores, nay hundreds, of the boys who have passed through this training ship, will lend the public to give the Captain and his Officers not a certain measure of sympathy, but their full and hearty support with the noble rescue work which I am convinced by direct personal knowledge goes on in this institution. Let the public remember what you so justly state, that "incidents of this kind might as easily happen in the army or in a public school", and then let them contrast the material there with what passes through our hands here.

I quite agree with the suggestion that some degree of classification might be attempted, to prevent the very worst boys from contaminating the rest, but this is a problem equally pressing of solution both in our work houses and prisons, and the early attention of the Government now in power, should be urged to this problem by all those interested in remedial measures for the elevation of this unfortunate stratum of our population.'

The same issue of the Chronicle refers in its Editorial column to the 'Clio Incident'. It concludes that 'Captain Langdon and his staff may be trusted to spare no effort to ensure the strictest discipline and exemplary conduct amongst the boys, and to see that serious offences do not go unpublished.'

In a letter to the Inspector of Reformatory and Industrial

Schools, dated 9th March, 1906, Captain Langdon expressed that his Committee had advised him to consult his solicitor about having charges brought against Slingsby, Meredith, Francis, Manley, Singleton and Forster, following the fatal bullying of William Crook. Mr Thornton Jones, the Captain's Solicitor, unfortunately, was of the opinion that there were no grounds for a prosecution under Rule 38 of the Rules and Bylaws of the ship, which could be made available as an offence within Section 32 of the Industrial Schools Act, 1866.

Captain Langdon was of the opinion that it was important to get rid of these young bullies, who were having a bad influence on the other 'Clio' boys, and whose committal to a Reformatory would have a most salutory effect on the general conduct. The Captain complained that his Punishment Book showed a list of 34 cases in six weeks as compared with nine in any previous similar period since he had been in command of the 'Clio'.

The five boys who had been mixed up in the bullying incident had since then been kept 'isolated as far as possible during play-time, but in spite of all precautions Singleton, Meredith and Slingsby have again been guilty of bullying since the inquest on their late victim (Slingsby several time).' Moreover, Slingsby and a boy named John Forester had trumped-up a false and malicious story against one of the seamen instructors in the hope of getting him into trouble. Captain Langdon describes Forester as 'a dwarf with a vicious disposition and a violent temper. He has on at least two occasions within the last six months narrowly missed hitting boys in the eyes with sharp implements and on the first of these occasions he (to avoid punishment) simulated blindness so cleverly that he deceived us all including the doctor.'

The Under Secretary of State replied to Captain Langdon's letter on 16th March, 1906, 'With reference to your letter of the 9th instant relative to the question of dealing with the boys implicated in the death of William Crook, I am directed by the

Secretary of State to say, for the information of your Committee, that he is of the opinion that Slingsby, Meredith, Singleton, Forster, Francis and Manley must be removed from the 'Clio'.

Mr Gladstone thinks that proceedings should at once be taken against all these boys (except Meredith and Slingsby who are under 15) either under Section 32 of the Industrial Schools Act, 1866, or Section 1 of the Reformatory Schools Act, 1893, for assault, with a view to committee to a Reformatory. If Meredith and Slingsby are not prosecuted, immediate efforts should be made to find Industrial Schools willing to take them if they are transferred by the Secretary of State. The Inspector would be prepared to render any assistance in his power in this matter.

The Secretary of State regrets to hear that there has been further bullying in the school, and will be glad to receive a detailed report of the facts at your early convenience.'

Captain Langdon and his Committee wasted no time and the *North Wales Chronicle* of 30th March, 1906, carries a report of 'Assaults on the "Clio" Training Ship', which resulted in George Singleton, John Forster and Albert Slingsby being summoned for assault before the Magistrates at Bangor Police Court on the previous Tuesday.

Mr Thornton Jones prosecuted on behalf of the authorities of the 'Clio'. The first case dealt with was that of Singleton, who, said Mr Thornton Jones, seized a fellow shipmate named Rowland Jones by the head, and barged it against the bulkhead of the ship. The solicitor did not intend to do anything more than roughly detail the facts of each case, and then if the magistrates were satisfied that the charges had been substantiated, he would give them some information which might affect the manner in which the boys could be punished. If the cases had been solitary ones they would have been dealt with on board, and the boys punished there and then. The proceedings had been brought with due deliberation, and with the sanction and by the direction of those who were responsible

153

for the well-being of the Industrial and Reformatory Schools of the country. The 'Clio' was not a Reformatory School, and none of the boys on board had been convicted. In order that the boys charged might have every fair play the authorities had communicated with their parents and guardians, and afforded them every opportunity of calling any witness they might wish.

Singleton had no one appearing for him. Both his parents were dead, and a letter from the Leigh Education Authority had been received suggesting that he might be sent to a Reformatory.

Rowland Jones, aged eleven, in his evidence stated that on 12th February, he had acted as night watchboy, and had received orders to call Singleton, but he would not get up from bed. Jones had gone for Mr Bray, the night watchman, who had turned Singleton out. He could not remember what the actual time was, except that it was during the middle watch, between midnight and four a.m. When Singleton had assaulted him Jones complained to another boy, name Keyers, who had taken him along to Mr Booth, Chief Officer on the 'Clio'. The Chief Officer then relieved Jones of his duties for the night.

The second charge of assault was preferred against John Forster, aged 15, 'whose dwarfish appearance caused some amusement to the habitues of the court'. Mr Thornton Jones said that Forster had thrown a hand scrubbing brush at a lad named Wright, severely cutting his face below his eye. The assault was a serious one, and had the brush been aimed a little higher, it would have destroyed the boy's eye. In reply to a letter informing him of the decision of the authorities to prosecute Forster, his father, who lived in Warrington, replied to the effect that he was not in a position to defend the case.

The third case was against Albert Slingsby, who was charged with assaulting Rowland Jones. Slingsby and four other boys had been kept apart from the rest of the boys, and it was Jones's duty, as cook of the mess, to take him his dinner. Slingsby had complained that there was not sufficient potatoes for him and struck Jones. The matter had been reported to the officers and since then a bigger boy had taken Slingsby his dinner.

Giving the decision of the Bench, the Chairman said that the Magistrates had unanimously come to the conclusion that the three boys had been guilty of assaults upon their comrades, and had decided that they should be sent to a Reformatory for three years.

Mr Thornton Jones informed the court that 'the authorities of the ship had found three different Reformatories where the boys could be sent to, and the Bench agreed that they should be sent to those institutions.' In order to save the boys from being sent to prison Captain Langdon promised to detain them on the 'Clio' until they were ready to be sent to the Reformatories.

The Editorial column of the *North Wales Chronicle* was again ready to come to the defence of the 'Clio', stating that 'the proceedings before the magistrates this week show that the authorities of the ship are quite determined to put down this reprehensible practice of 'ragging' with a stern hand.' Concluding that 'now the incident is closed, Bangorians will hope that the ship will pursue the even tenour of her way, and long continue to do the good work in the Menai Strait where she forms so striking a feature, and whence she sends forth her sons to swell the ranks of British sailors, both mercantile and naval. Such institutions can ill be spared as any student of maritime economics know so well.'

Although the *North Wales Chronicle* thought the incident was closed, it was not. Mr Osmond Williams had tabled a question in the House of Commons for 9th April, 1906. It was 'To ask the Secretary of State for the Home Department, whether he can now give the result of his inquiries into the case of death resulting from bullying on board the 'Clio'.'

The Secretary of State before answering the question requested that the Inspector of Reformatory and Industrial Schools submit a report 'on the discipline maintained on board the 'Clio', showing whether in the Inspector's opinion any of the officers were in any way to blame for what occurred, either on the score of neglect at the time of the incident, or of general laxity in maintaining discipline." Whilst waiting for this report from the Inspector the Secretary of State had asked Mr Osmond Williams to postpone his question until after the Easter recess.

The Bishop of Bangor, one of the 'Clio's' managers, who was constantly on board, according to the Inspector, had gone into the matter of bullying on the ship very carefully with some of his colleagues was 'emphatic in cleaning the officers of blame.'

Mr Legge, the Inspector, in his report, informed the Secretary of State that Captain Langdon had been in charge of the 'Clio' for some five years. 'He succeeded a Capt. Moger, R.N., whose views of discipline were in my opinion too strict, and I have rendered Capt. Langdon all the support in my power in introducing a milder discipline.' According to Mr Legge, 'the inquiry in January interfered seriously with the discipline on board, for, as a result of misadventure which it is perhaps unnecessary to describe afresh, Capt. Langdon received no intimation of the inquiry. The boys, very quick in apprehension of such matters, saw that the inquiry was sprung on him, and jumped to the conclusion that the Capt. and Officers were on their trial.' He concluded by stating that 'with open weather and consequently regular hard work in the boats it will be found in a month or six weeks that no one can pick a hole in this as compared with any other of the ships certified by the Secretary of State. The Managers are wide awake, and they as well as the Captain have fine support in the Chaplain.'

The Secretary of State showed Mr Legge's report to Mr Osmond Williams, who thought it unnecessary to put any further questions, and someone from the Home Office saw fit to add to the bottom of the report – 'All's well that ends well.'

The adverse publicity that the 'Clio' had received during the early part of 1906 had brought doubts into people's minds about the discipline maintained on board. Sir Horatio Lloyd, Clerk of the Peace for Cheshire, speaking at Knutsford Quarter Sessions, after reporting that eleven Cheshire boys had been sent to the 'Clio', summed it all up when he said that he did not 'think it was possible to have a more humane or satisfactory officer in charge of such a ship than the Superintendent, Captain Langdon. He was the perfection of an officer to be in charge of the ship, and both he and his wife had the interests of the boys entirely at heart. The incident in question happened whilst an officer's back was turned for a minute, and the poor boy, probably little more than half-witted, had his head knocked against a projected piece of wood, from the effect of which he died. The three boys responsible for the affair had since been sent by the magistrate to separate Reformatories for three years, and the ship had been relieved of a very undesirable element. There was no occasion to apprehend that anything of the kind would occur there again.'

Despite the tragic start to the year 1906 life on board the 'Clio' continued as usual. The physical training was now 'on the Swedish lines adopted by the Royal Navy', and Band was 'excellent', and although the general standard of education was only 'very fair', the schoolroom staff were now settled and 'next year's work show solid advance.' The Inspector believed that a cloud had passed over the 'Clio' during the year, and bullying by a handful of ill-conditioned lads, however carefully watched, was dangerous in any kind of school. Despite this, 'The ship's prestige should still receive as clear recognition as in the past.'

CHAPTER 14

1907 until the outbreak of the First World War

The 'Clio' was inspected twice during 1907, on the 1st May and 13th September. Since the tragic bullying incident of 1906, many staff changes had taken place. Mr Booth, the Chief Officer, had left in November, 1906, and had been replaced by Mr George Tremayne in December. The first assistant schoolmaster, Mr Robinson, had left in June, 1906, to be succeeded by Mr H. C. Philip, who left in October, 1906, to be replaced by Mr W. Gastall in January, 1907. Mr Luxton, second assistant schoolmaster, left in December, 1906, to be replaced by Mr J. Evans. Mr Roach, the cook, died in January, 1907, and was succeeded by Mr Dickenson. The gunnery instructor left in March, 1907, and furthermore, the staff had been reduced by two seamen instructors, carpenter and swimming instructor.

Several improvements had been made to the ship during the year. The schoolroom work was now done on the upper deck; the space occupied by the lamp room had been fitted up for manual instruction, and a new store room had been made for school gear. The ship had been presented with a large globe and some nautical instruments by a well-wisher.

The general educational standard was still only 'fair' due to the many staff changes, but the Inspector expected improvements in the coming year. No formal technical instruction was given in tailoring or shoe-making, but eight boys assisted the ship's carpenter. Captain Langdon took a recreation class in carving and Mrs Langdon took a class in knitting. Cricket and football were played ashore at least twice a week, according to the season. Rifle practice took place on the lawn of the Bishop of Bangor's Palace; the Bishop himself having provided the rifles, and converted his lawn into a small rifle range.

The general health on board the 'Clio' was described as being 'good' apart from a few skin complaints. A boy had fallen overboard in February, but had been rescued by the Chief Officer, who received the Humane Society's medal. Conduct had been 'quite good' apart from a boy of roving tendencies endeavouring to run away, and to take another with him, but both were brought back. Five boys had been involved in setting a boat adrift, and there were the usual cases of pilfering food, being in forbidden quarters, and smoking.

1908 followed the same trend with an epidemic of influenza in February, which affected 70 boys and several officers. A boy had absconded from the Liverpool Home after signing for sea. There had been three of four attempts to run away from the ship, one of breaking leave, several cases of bad language and habits, and the usual smoking offences.

In 1909, of the 134 boys on board, and who were over 13 years of age, 78 received instruction in seamanship, and 17 others in tailoring shoe-making or carpentering. Of the remainder twelve were in the Band, but there were 17 who received full time education in the schoolroom, and of the 75 boys that had left the ship during the year 49 had gone to sea.

Health problems during 1909 were more numerous than for many years. Two new boys, who should possibly not have been admitted, died, one in January from an effusion on the brain, and one in March from enteritis. Two boys were transferred to shore schools as being unfit for sea life. There were two cases of diptheria and 20 cases of mumps, followed by an epidemic of chicken pox which affected 150 boys.

During his inspection of the 'Clio' on the 26th and 27th July, and 26th October, 1910, the Inspector found the ship to be 'very clean and in good order throughout.' New instruments had been purchased for the Band. There had been two deaths since the previous inspection, one from pneumonia and the other from acute rheumatism. One boy developed scarlet fever and thirteen others were affected. The boys had been to camp in December, 1909, which gave the authorities an opportunity to fumigate the ship. Whilst at camp a boy had run away and broken into a house nearby; an offence which resulted in him being transferred to a Reformatory.

Although the ship was visited by the Departmental Medical Adviser, who reported favourable on its condition and on the care taken of the boys, the Inspector in his report for 1911 states that there was one death from cerebro-spinal meningitis. During the year there had been four cases of chicken pox, one of measles, three of tonsilitis, four of mumps, and eleven cases of gastric catarrh. Despite this the boys had done well at the annual inspection and the improvement in their work noticed the previous year had been more than maintained.

In his report for 1912, the Inspector, Mr J. C. Pearson, states that one of the 'Clio' boys was knocked down by a motor car whilst marching with the Band and received serious injuries, the effects of which were likely to be permanent. Three new boys 'in a spirit of mischief, which fortunately had no serious consequences, let one of their number over the ship's side.' Mr Pearson was, however, happy to report that by now the 'Clio has a definite place in the social life of the locality, and the boys frequently take part in public functions, and so come into contact with outside influences and experience which assist materially in brightening them and in maintaining the tone and spirit of the school.'

The recommendations of the Department Committee of 1913 on Schools in England and Wales were brought into effect during 1914. This meant that the Division of the Home Office which had formerly dealt with the administration of the Children Act together with many other subjects, was relieved of practically all its work except questions relating to children. Under the new organisation this Children's Division dealt with Reformatory and Industrial Schools, questions relating to the protection and prevention of cruelty to children, juvenile courts, and administration of the Employment of Children Act, and questions connected with probation officers appointed under the Probation of Offenders Act.

Arrangements had been made with the Board of Education for the co-operation of their Inspectors in the inspection of Reformatory and Industrial Schools on the lines recommended by the Committee. The Committee's recommendation that there should be a superannuation scheme for all officers of the schools had been accepted, and a Departmental Committee had been appointed to prepare a scheme under Section 56 of the Children Act.

A full-time Medical Inspector and an additional woman Inspector with medical qualifications had been added to the staff of the Department. Unfortunately the newly appointed Medical Inspector, Dr. A. H. Norris, had only taken up his new duties a month or two before the First World War broke out, when he was called to the Colours.

A special form had been issued on which Medical Officers were required to make their quarterly reports, and new forms of Medical and Dental Record approved by the Medical Inspector had been prepared, and published by the Reformatory and Refuge Union. 76 schools had already adopted the new Medical Record Cards, and 43 the Dental Record Cards, replacing books which did not give all the particulars required by the Medical Inspector.

The Treasury had accepted the Committee's recommendation that the annual grants should be received by £50,000. The Finance Bill of 1914, as originally introduced, also contained provision for an additional £22,000, which would have been utilised for the relief of local authorities by increasing the Treasury grants for Education Act cases, but unfortunately the part of the Bill containing this provision had to be abandoned.

During 1913 and 1914 many structural improvements were carried out on the 'Clio'. New fresh water tanks had been put in the ship, allowing for the storage of 20 tons of water, instead of 12 tons as formerly. Fourteen wash basins had been provided on the main deck, and a set of post office telegraph apparatus, and a wireless buzzer and receiver had been installed, to enable the boys to practice the preliminaries of wireless telegraphy. A new telephone had also been installed, but some of the boys had seen fit to cut the wires, an offence for which they were punished.

With the outbreak of the First World War schools saw their staffs depleted in some cases to vanishing point. The 'Clio' had ten of its staff mobilised immediately, and in the figures given by the Chief Inspector in his 59th Annual Report, it appears that nine of these served in the Royal Navy and one in the Army. Of the number of boys enlisted in HM Forces between 4th August 1914 and 1st March 1916, 124 ex-'Clio' boys were in the Army and 122 in the Royal Navy. As the Flag Captain at Portsmouth had informed Captain Langdon in a letter, 'I shall want all the boys the ship can send, as the 'Clio' is the only sure and satisfactory supply I have.'

Chapter 15

The First World War and the end of the 'Clio'

The Great War, as it was known, marked the close of a decade of great and fruitful activity in every field of education. During the first twelve months of war the Board of Education was fully occupied in ensuring 'that the system was carried on as far as possible without interruption and with undiminished efficiency.' As Graves continues, 'It is typical of the general unpreparedness of the country for war that no plans had been made in advance for dealing with the inevitable problems of staffing, while the commandeering of 743 schools for military purposes and another 80 or so for hospitals added to the Board's embarrassment.' The Reformatory and Industrial Schools were not to be left out of the 'war-effort', and their participation in munition work originated in June, 1915, when the Minister of Munitious agreed with the Secretary of State that the inmates of these schools might 'usefully engage in this form of national service.'

Although the 'Clio' is not specifically mentioned in the Inspector's Appendix on 'Munition Work' in his 59th Annual Report, it is interesting to note that the tendency is still there to make full use of these boys and girls as a form of cheap labour. The Inspector states that 'about 50 boys at a time from the National Nautical School have been employed since April, 1915, in filling petrol tins for the Asiatic Petrol Co., Portishead. Altogether 250 individual boys have been engaged from this school, and £2,200 has been earned in wages, of which half has gone to the boys and the other half to the general school funds.'

The type of work carried out by the other children was as varied as it was dangerous. Kibble had 56 boys working at Messrs Beardmore's Paisley Shell Factory, six others in a hand-grenade factory, three with a mine-sweeper firm, twelve on the manufacture of poison gases and explosives, and five with a firm making munition boxes. Parkhead had 18 boys at Beardmore's (Parkhead) Shell Factory, and another 25 with Messrs Mavor and Coulson, Glasgow. In addition 'flying squads' of boys had been requisitioned by this firm in emergency times of loading up shells in transport wagons, off-loading at the railway depot and re-loading into railway trucks. Some hundreds of boys from the Ilford, East London, Field Lane, Dartford, Chelmsford and LCC Industrial Schools had been employed in Woolwich Arsenal on the production of rifle cartridges.

The Norton Boys Home had been involved in less dangerous work, and had produced in a year, 5,000 despatch-riders' kit covers, 2,500 bandoliers, 2,500 buckle straps stitched on, 3,400 ammunition pouches, 1,579 water bottle carriers, and 295 flag-signallers' cases. The Church Farm Industrial School had shaped 90,000 tooth brush handles for military use, and had also made 2,500 splints as well as box 'tidies' for VAD Hospitals.

The Warwick Girls Reformatory School stitched 100,000 web loops for 1,816 shells in five months. The Thorparch Girls Industrial School had made 5,000 medical pads, 9,000 signalling flags and 1,500 flags of various nations.

In addition to this, 6,957 boys from the Reformatory Schools and 109 staff had enlisted in HM Forces; and from the eleven Industrial Schools 2,767 boys and 49 staff had enlisted by 1st March, 1916.

With the reduction in his staff Capital Langdon found 'the work had been rather arduous since the war broke out.' He had given one boy, whose time had expired, the position of an officer, and the more competent of the older boys he had made Instructors, and they were all doing well.

On the 5th June, 1914, the boys were taken to camp at Llandudno for four weeks; the North Wales Steamship Company 'with their usual generosity' conveying them there and back free of charge. On the 30th July, the Diocesan Inspector examined the boys, and his report shows that he was satisfied with their knowledge of the Scriptures. Prior to this 24 boys had been baptised at St Mary's Church, Bangor, on 7th April, and 90 boys had been confirmed by the Bishop of Bangor on 8th April.

Although there is very little printed evidence available, the 'Clio's' time was drawing to a close. The problems brought on by the First World War, no doubt, accelerated the decision to close the school, besides the fact that the ship's timbers were by now in the last stages of rotting. Staff problems continued to the end, when the National Service Representative appealed against the exemption given Edwin Pritchard, the tailor instructor, and J. Elias Jones, assistant schoolmaster, both classed as Grade I. However, both appeals were disallowed at the Aethwy Tribunal, and the absolute exemption granted on 29th February, 1918, was confirmed.

The Band continued to play and march at all the local major events, such as the consecration of Church Island, Menai Bridge, in August, 1918. With Armistice Day on 11th November, 1918, the 'Clio' boys and their Band were well to the fore at the Thanksgiving Service held at Bangor Cathedral later in the month.

The 'Clio' ceased to be an Industrial School in May, 1919, when the Managers resigned the Certificate of the School. The Education Act of 1918, also, must have played its part in the closing of the 'Clio' as well as other Industrial Schools. Although there were no provisions in the Act expressly affecting Reformatory and Industrial Schools, the Chief Inspector for Reformatory and Industrial Schools in his letter to the Managers and Staff of these schools, believed that 'these schools must necessarily raise their standards and modify their methods in harmony with changes in the national system of which they are parts.'

The 1918 Education Act abolished the old provisions under which children might spend half time at work and half time at school, and required all children under 14 (15 if the Local Education Authority fixed this higher age) to attend school full time. Moreover, it closely limited the employment of children before and after school hours. Although these provisions did not extend to children in Reformatory and Industrial Schools, it was clearly incumbent on the Managers of such schools at see that children under their care were no worse off than other children. The object of restricting the employment of children was to ensure that the child in school should, with untried faculties, be able to profit to the full from the education provided. This consideration was as applicable to the children in Home Office schools as to other children, and it had to be borne in mind that though useful employment or useful work (at the proper times and properly restricted) was good, it was bad if it enroached on the time that should be given to organised training or healthy recreation.

The Chief Inspector believed that the main defects of the Reformatory and Industrial Schools was 'that the children spend too much time in occupations which, though not necessarily bad in themselves, prevent the child spending his time and energies in ways that are educationally better. Every useful task, if it is only sweeping the yard or running an errand, may have some educational value, but in mapping out the children's days, the question each Superintendent should put to himself is not 'Has such and such a task some educational value?' but 'Is this the best form of occupation that can be provided? Is the best use being made of the time at my disposal for the education of the child?'

The Pwllheli Guardians were at least concerned about the closing of the 'Clio'. Through Major Breese, MP, they asked the Home Secretary about the possibility of establishing an Industrial School in North Wales to replace the 'Clio'. The Home Secretary, however, did not believe that the number of committees to Industrial Schools from the area did not justify the establishing of such a school in North Wales to receive Welsh speaking boys. There was, he said in his reply to Major Breese, an Industrial School in Swansea to which Welsh boys could be sent.

Captain Langdon resigned his position as Honorary Secretary of the Royal Anglsey Yacht Club in October, 1919. He had been the Club's Honorary Secretary for twelve years, and for his services he was elected a Life Member of the Club.

On Sunday, 21st March, 1920, the 'Clio' was towed to the Christiana jetty 'to be scuttled and broken up for firewood.' A suggestion has been made that Bangor City Council should 'endeavour to acquire the figure-head of the old ship for the museum.' By 1st April the 'Clio's' masts had been taken down, and fifteen men were at work dismantling the ship. Messrs Owen and Lloyd, Bangor, carried out a public auction of all the useful parts of the 'Clio' at the Christiana Yard, Garth Point, Bangor, on Friday, 16th April 1920.

On 7th April, 1920 an Order was made by the Board of Education, under the Charitable Trusts Acts 1853 to 1894, in the Matter of the Endowment of the North Wales, City of Chester and Border Counties Industrial School Training Ship Society commonly known as the Society of the Industrial Training Ship 'Clio' lately stationed off Bangor, North Wales. Gratuities were handed out to the fifteen members of the Clio's staff, totalling £2,628, and ranging from £1,000 for Captain Langdon to £20 for Mr James Lee, the Head Schoolmaster.

The Hayley and Clio Educational Fund is still in being and looked after by Warmsley, Henshall and Co., Chartered

Accountants, Chester, who are the Secretaries to the Trust, and use is still made of the funds to assist orphaned children in the North Wales and Cheshire areas.

Chapter 16

Conclusion

According to David Thomson, the main motif of the Nineteenth Century was 'the remarkable accumulation of material wealth and power which the English people achieved during the century.' It was a century that saw a revolution in government. In a predominantly rural society, it had been sufficient to provide such services as education, the maintenance of law and order, the relief of the poor, and the upkeep of the King's highway on a local and voluntary basis. Industrialisation and urbanisation made these methods obsolete. They had to be replaced by institutions and bureaucracies that were under the control of the central government. In the course of this process new departments of state, of which the Education Department was one amongst many had to be set up and extra duties had to be given to existing government offices.

The accumulation of the wealth and power of the period was to many Englishmen hidden from view and they were completely unconscious of many of the very foundations of this power. 'The world-wide power of the City of London, for example was as discreetly veiled from public view as the legs of mid-Victorian pianos; the supremacy of the British Navy was normally as silent as footsteps upon the layers of drawing room carpets. And, because the nakedness of power was withheld form view, men for long periods forgot how necessary this basis of power was to the whole structure of English greatness. It was, paradoxically, when this power was crumbling that Englishmen began to talk about it – and even to brandish it – most.'

In the 1850s and 60s, despite her great technological lead in industry and her vast merchant navy, Britain did not originate any of the great naval developments. The days of sail were numbered and Britain initiated changes introduced by France and the United States of America, and initiated so clumsily that naval shipbuilding passed through a baroque phase. For example, the 'Warrior', though built of iron, was a full-rigged steam-and-sail ship with three masts and a bowsprit, carrying her guns on the broadside.

However, Great Britain throughout the hey-day of mid-Victorian prosperity kept up a large and costly fleet, in fact, the biggest in the world. On this fleet she implicitly pinned her faith for complete national defence. 'The fleet in being was a permanent factor in her whole position, both in Europe and as a maritime Empire. It was ever the framework for her policy of free trade, for it and nothing else ensured for all the freedom of the seas.'

The concern of a maritime Empire about the manning of its navy, both Royal and mercantile, combined with the problem of pauperism and juvenile crime amongst the seething mass at the foot of the social ladder, gave the government of the time, with the aid of the essential philanthropic gentlemen, the ideal opportunity of solving both problems by establishing Industrial Training Ships. Unfortunately these were not to be the success they were expected to be, because the majority of the boys sent to the ships were completely unsuited for life at sea, being mentally, physically and emotionally retarded. In addition the stigma of the boys' criminal connections however slight or indirect was sufficient to bar them from entering the Royal Navy. There were continual complaints about the number of boys actually taking up a sea life as a career during the whole of the time the 'Clio' was in existence as an Industrial Training Ship. There was very little doubt, however, that the 'Clio' provided a fairly reasonable standard of education and training for her boys at this time, as many poor respectable parents were to complain of the opportunities offered to these destitute boys as being superior to that offered their children.

Life on board the 'Clio' was, to say the least, difficult and harsh. The exposed position of the ship meant that it was open to all types of weather, and consequently there were the inevitable illnesses, accidents and deaths. Although the life was hard, to many of the boys educated on the 'Clio' it was the nearest they had seen to a home, and from the many letters the boys wrote back to the masters after leaving the ship they obviously thought highly of her and the staff.

After the Boer War various committees established to enquire into the state of health of the nation revealed, amongst other things, the high level of physical unfitness among army recruits. The reports of these committees also indicated that many elementary school children were under-fed. In turn these reports lead to the foundation of the Health Service and a School Meals Service which inevitably had an effect on the Reformatory and Industrial Training Schools.

From 1906 to 1916 the Liberals formed the government of the day and were responsible for bringing in major social legislation. After 1902 there were various consolidating pieces of educational legislation that finally accumulated in the Fisher Education Act of 1918.

With the 'war to end all wars' of 1914-18 came the 'writing on the wall' for the 'Clio'. Although like the elementary schools the 'Clio' and other Industrial Training Ships were to prove their worth on the battlefield before long, it was actually the ravages of time and the weather that were to bring the 'Clio' to a close. This closure was inevitably accelerated by the Education Act of 1918 and the eventual improvements in life in general with the coming of the Welfare State.

That the 'Clio' did to a great extent play the part it was

171

intended to, is best summed up by 'A.R.D.' an ex-'Clio' boy writing from Shotley Barracks, Harwich, during the first year of the 1914-18 war:

'The 'Clio' was the boat that I learnt all my seamanship and gunnery in, and it has helped me on a lot, so that when I joined to the R.N. I knew nearly all my work. Everything about seamanship and signals and gunnery; the same that is taught on board the 'Clio' is just the same as is taught today in the R.N. I must now close with an old boy's love for his ship. – I am, your obedient servant, A.R.D.'

APPENDIX 1

The industrial training ships and reformatories

The extent of the training ship system, when nearly complete, is indicated in the following figures taken from a Parliamentary Paper, 8th February, 1875 and quoted by E. C. Millington in 'Seamen in the Making – A Short History of Nautical Training'.

Name	Accommodation	Number on board on 1st Sept., 1874
Akbar	200	170
Clarence	250	229
Cornwall	250	238
Cumberland	360	349
Endeavour	150	149
Formidable	325	297
Gibraltar	350	214
Havannah	100	84
Mars	300	305
Southampton	240	200
Wellesley	300	278
Other training ships:		
Chichester	200	250
Goliath	500	399
Indefatigable	250	149
Warspite	200	200
TOTALS:	3,975	3,511

Akbar: Established 1856, on the River Mersey, near Rock Ferry, Birkenhead.

Reformatory for criminals. No boys received except under

sentence of magistrate. Boys were committed for 5 years, but normally remained for a little over 3 years. Minimum age of joining the ship was 12 years, maximum 16 years. Minimum and maximum age for leaving the ship was 15 and 19 years old, depending upon conduct; the authorities had the power to put the boys out on licence after 18 months detention. The original 'Akbar' was HMS 'Cornwallis', an East Indiaman of 1,363 tons, renamed 'Akbar' in 1812 and used for quarantine service at Liverpool from 1827 to 1855. Only a short period elapsed before she was replaced in May 1862, by the 'Wellington', which took her name of 'Akbar'. This ship was a third-rate frigate built in 1816, of 1,757 tons, and was retained in service as a training ship until 1908, when she was condemned as unfit for further service, broken up and replaced by a shore establishment.

Clarence: Established 15th August, 1864, on the River Mersey, near Rock Ferry, Birkenhead. Reformatory. Minimum and maximum age for joining the ship was 12 and 16 years. No minimum and maximum leaving age. The ship was run by the Liverpool Committee of the Catholic Reformatory Association. The movement to provide a Catholic reformatory ship was commenced in 1863, and in 1864 the Admiralty loaned HMS Clarence, an 84 gun line-of-battle ship. Boys remained on the average about three years, and about 90 per cent of them went to sea. Round about 1880 a mutiny occurred among the boys who made attempts to set fire to the vessel. A few years later on 17th January, 1884, the 'Clarence' boys succeeded in burning their ship. It was suspected that the boys stole small quantities of oil as opportunity presented itself, and with this they gradually soaked a sail in the sail locker in the hold, setting fire to this when it was saturated. Though she was replaced by another 'Clarence', a repetition of the mischief occurred, and on 26th July, 1899, the boys again fired the vessel. There was no loss of life, however, when the ship was destroyed. It was resolved for a number of reasons not to apply for another ship, and a school was established on shore to take its place. This school was called the Farnworth Nautical School, and was built near Widnes, the boys being transferred. After some years the nautical instruction was discontinued because there were no facilities for it at the school, which was at some considerable distance from the river. The Farnworth School still existed in 1935 as a Catholic reformatory, its name being Farnworth St Aidan's School, and it received junior boys only. The original certificate continued in force for the reformatory at that time.

Cornwall: Established June 1859, off Purfleet, Essex. Reformatory. The 'Cornwall' was still in being in 1935 according to Millington. The boys remained about three years, entering between 11 and 15 years of age. The establishment was maintained by government grants, county and borough payments in respect of individual boys and voluntary contributions.

Cumberland: Certified as an Industrial Training School 30th June, 1869, Moored in Row Bay, Gareloch, Dumbartonshire. An article from the 'Glasgow Herald', 20th March, 1891, reads as follows:

"On 5th November, 1868, about a dozen prominent Glasgow gentlemen, under the presidency of Mr (now Sir) John Burns (afterwards Lord Inverclyde), met in the Underwriter's committee room with the view of establishing and maintaining a training ship on the Clyde for homeless and destitute boys under the provisions of the Industrial Schools Act of 1866. The first object in view was to provide a home for the reception, education and training of boys, who, through poverty or parental neglect, or being orphans, or who from any other cause were left destitute and homeless and in danger of being contaminated by association with vice and crime, a subsidiary object being towards aiding in the supply of young men specially trained as sailors for the naval and mercantile marine of the country. In this way two great wants would be brought together and satisfied – the rescuing of our street arabs and an increase to the number and efficiency of our seamen. A large general committee, Mr Burns being President, with an efficient executive, the late Mr James Galbraith being Chairman, having been appointed, steps were immediately taken for carrying out these objects, the institution being named 'The Clyde Industrial Training Ship Association'. As regards the main object, on enquiry it was found that besides boys who had passed entirely beyond the control of their parents our streets afforded abundant scope for such an institution, numberless destitute boys, utterly uneducated, many of them homeless and parentless, obtaining what food they could get by receiving alms or begging under the pretence of selling or offering small things, such at matches, for sale, and finding shelter during the night, in winter as well as in summer, by laying themselves down, wretchedly clothed as they were, in stains, closes, closets and other altogether unsuitable outhouses. Application having been made to the Home Office, the Admiralty and the Treasury on the subject of a grant of a ship, the committee, after considerable negotiations, had the satisfaction a few months afterwards of being informed that the Admiralty had granted the use of HMS 'Cumberland', 2,114 tons, then lying at Sheerness, for the purpose of the institution. A considerable sum of money being required to bring round the 'Cumberland' to the Clyde, to alter, fit her up and furnish her, and to provide for the expenditure connected with establishing the institution, an appeal was made to the sympathies of the large mercantile and shipping communities of the Clyde ports. The 'Cumberland' having been brought round, was moored off Row, in the Ganeloch. It was fitted up and duly certified as an industrial training ship under the Act. At the end of 1869 there were 174 boys on board and about 400 at the end of each of the following years down to the commencement of 1889. The unfortunate destruction of the 'Cumberland' by fire in the spring of 1889 fell somewhat suddenly upon the committee, but did not paralyse their efforts. On the contrary, they at once proceeded to replace their great loss. The committee, having made application for another ship, have been fortunate in securing the use of HMS 'Revenge', which for some years past has been stationed at Queenstown as the Admiral's flagship on the Irish station. As the Admiralty proposes to build another ship of that name, the committee was asked to rechristen her, and she was accordingly, with the sanction of the Admiralty, renamed 'Empress'. She has since been removed from Queenstown to the Clyde, and is now at the old moorings of the 'Cumberland' off Row in the Ganeloch. She is a magnificent wooden two-decker of larger size than her predecessor and well worthy of a visit. To alter her properly and fit her up has entailed a very large expense upon the Executive Committee. To raise the sum necessary they have resolved to appear to the generosity of the public, and they trust the inhabitants of Glasgow, Greenock and other coast towns in the Clyde district appreciating their efforts in the past on behalf of the poor outcast boys, will respond to the appeal they have resolved to make."

This is truly indicative, as with the establishment of the 'Clio', of the part played by private endeavour in the betterment of social conditions, a spirit which it has always been the object of English administration to foster.

The 'Empress', as she was now known, closed as an industrial training ship on 30th June, 1923.

Endeavour: Certified as an industrial school on 18th July, 1866. Land training brig at Middlesex Industrial School, Feltham, near Hounslow. The 'Endeavour' was a model ship, consisting of the deck and masts of a vessel fully brig-rigged, on which instruction in seamanship was given. Boat work was carried out at Walton-on-Thames. The school was supported by a county rate and was under the control of the magistrates of the county who appointed a committee of visitors, a system which continued until 1889, in which year the school was transferred to the LCC by the Local Government Act. It was finally closed down in 1909.

Formidable: Certified as an industrial training school 29th November, 1869, off Portishead, Somerset. Eventually became a shore establishment known as the National Nautical School, Portishead.

Gibraltar: Certified as an industrial training school 7th June, 1872. Moored off Belfast, Northern Ireland.

Havannah: Certified as an industrial training school in 1861. Stationed Grange Road, Cardiff.

Mars: Certified as an industrial training school 30th September, 1869. Stationed in the River Tay, about 2 miles from the Port of Dundee. Eventually became a hostel and closed down in 1935.

Southampton: Certified as an industrial training school 24th September, 1868. Stationed off Hull. The first fourteen boys on board had been transferred from the Hull Ragged and Industrial Schools. The ship left Hull on 10th July, 1912, having been sold by the Admiralty to be broken up.

Wellesley: Certified as an industrial training school 17th January, 1868. Stationed off Shields, River Tyne. Eventually became the shore establishment, Wellesley Nautical School, Blyth, Newcastle.

Chichester: Established December, 1866 at Greenhithe.

Goliath: Certified as an industrial training school 9th November, 1870.
Stationed off Grays, Essex. Its maintenance was furnished by the rules from the unions of Hackney, Poplar and Whitechapel, and attached to the Forest Gate district of the London School Board. Attached to the 'Goliath' was a tender, 'Steadfast', acquired in 1871 for seamanship instruction. A fire on board the vessel on 22nd December, 1875, resulted in the complete destruction of the old 'Goliath', and its place was taken in 1876 by the 'Exmouth' an old wooden line-of-battle ship dating from 1854. The control of the institution was then taken over by the Metropolitan Asylums Board since boys were being drawn from all the Metropolitan parishes. The wooden 'Exmouth' was replaced in 1905 by a vessel specially built to the order of the Board to accommodate 700 boys and 45 staff. She was an over-sized replica of the 'Victory', the dimensions being approximately twice those of the famous old ship.

Indefatigable: Certified in July 1865, mainly for the sons and orphans of sailors. Stationed on the River Mersey, Liverpool.

Warspite: Established 1756. The Warspite belonged to the Marine Society, which originated the training ship's system. All boys were subjected to a strict medical examination before admission, and engaged to serve wherever they were sent, whether Royal Navy or Merchant Service.

Mount Edgcumbe: Certified 1877, the last of the industrial training ships off the English coast. For nearly 44 years the ship was used as an industrial school for the counties of Devon and Cornwall, being moored in the Tamar just above Saltash Bridge. She was formerly the 'Winchester', which had served as the

'Conway' training ship from 1861 to 1867. In July 1876, she was handed over to the Devon and Cornwall Industrial Training Ship Association, and continued in service until 1920.

Shaftesbury: Certified 1877 off Grays, Essex. Founded by the London School Board. The vessel was bought from the P. & O. Company and was formerly the 'Nubia'. The 'Shaftesbury' had attached a topsail schooner 'Themis', a vessel of 145 tons. During the summer months the 'Thermis' cruised in the estuary of the Thames and down the channel as far as Plymouth; her complement on these trips was three officers and thirty boys.

APPENDIX 2

The 'Indefatigable"

School Number 573/5000.
Registered office:- Room 22, First Floor, Oriel Chambers,
14 Water Street, Liverpool.

from a letter to me from Mr R. N. Hatfield, Secretary, 15th
February, 1977.

"The 'Indefatigable' was moored off Rock Ferry from 1864 to
1913 when it was replaced by 'Phaeton', renamed 'Indefatigable',
which remained in the River Mersey until 1941, when the
Admiralty decided that due to enemy bombing of the docks,
'Indefatigable' would have to be evacuated.

'Indefatigable' was towed away to be broken up and the
School moved to a holiday camp in North Wales until 1944
when it was combined with the Liverpool Sea Training Homes
to become 'The Indefatigable and National Sea Training School
for Boys'.

The new school was shore based on the Menai Strait."

Bibliography

Public Record Office, London
65394 PRO HO 45/9553 Establishment of Training Ship 'Clio' – including questions of age limits of boys (1877-1882).
B19615 PRO HO 45/10413 'Clio' Industrial Training Ship.
Bullying by boys resulting in death of another boy (1900-1906).
B10432 PRO HO 45/9839 Reformatory and Industrial Schools Ships. Cooking by boys and training in the use of fuel (1891).
B8262E PRO HO 45/9822 (1-30)
9823 (31-onwards) Reformatory and Industrial Schools Ships.
General aspects and enquiries (1891-99).
Maritime Museum, London.
MSY/C/7. Minutes of the Marine Society Meetings.
Merseyside County Museums, Liverpool
John Smart Collection. Typed account of the 'Clio'.
H370 SCH. Proceedings of the Liverpool School Board (1877-8).
'Navy Lists' 1862-1874.
Home Office, London
Annual Reports of the Chief Inspector of Reformatory and Industrial Schools of Great Britain (1876-1916)
Clwyd Archives, Ruthin
Annual Reports of the Society of the Industrial Training Ship 'Clio'.
1882, 1883, 1884, 1886, 1887.
Agreement between the County of Denbighshire Magistrates and the Industrial Ship 'Clio', 1880.
Agreement between the Wrexham Union and the Industrial Training Ship 'Clio', 1880.
Gwynedd Archives, Caernarfon
Pwllheli Union Minute Book, 10th October 1917-11th January 1922.
Annual Reports of the Society of the Industrial Training Ship 'Clio', 1879, 1880, 1881.

William III A.D. 1696, Cap. XXI, An Act for the Increase and Encouragement of Seamen.

William III A.D. 1697, Cap. XXIII, An Act to Enforce the Act for the Increase and Encouragement of Seamen.

Anne, A.D. 1703, Cap. VI, An Act for the Increase of Seamen and better Encouragement of Navigation, and Security of the Coal Trade.

Victoria 17 & 18, Cap. LXXXVI (1854), An Act for the better care and Reformation of Youthful Offenders in Great Britain.

Victoria 19 & 20, Cap. CIX (1856), An Act to amend the Mode of Committing Criminal and Vagrant Children to Reformatory and Industrial Schools.

Victoria 23 & 24, Cap. CVIII (1860), An Act to amend the Industrial Schools Act 1857.

Victoria 24 & 25, Cap. CXIII (1861), An Act for amending and consolidating the Law relating to Industrial Schools.

Victoria 29 & 30, Cap. CXVII (1866), An Act to consolidate and amend the Acts relating to Reformatory Schools in Great Britain.

Victoria 29 & 30, Cap. CXVIII (1866), An Act to consolidate and amend the Acts relating to Industrial Schools in Great Britain.

1. Edward 7 (1901), Chapter 20, An Act to amend the Law relating to Youthful Offenders and for the purposes connected therewith.

8. Edward 7 (1908), Children's Act.

City of Chester Records Office
Scheme made by the Board of Education under the Charitable Trusts Act 1853 to 1894. Endowment of Training Ship 'Clio', 16 September, 1921.

Newspapers

North Wales Chronicle, 1876-1921	} Gwynedd Archives,
Caernarfon & Denbigh Herald, 1900-1920	} Caernarfon

Chester Chronicle   }
Cheshire Observer, 1875-1900   }
Chester Courant   }   Chester Public Library
Wrexham Leader   }

Liverpool Courier, 24 March, 1920. Brown Picton Library,
Liverpool
The Times, 14th February, 1906   }   Public Record
The Manchester Guardian, 12th February, 1906 }   Office, London

Books

Allen, B.M. 'Sir Robert Morant', Macmillan, 1934.
Banbury, Philip, 'Shipbuilders of the Thames and Medway',
David and Charles, Newton Abbot, 1971.
Barker, R., 'Education and Politics 1900-1951', Oxford
University Press, 1972.
Bass, G.F. (Editor), 'A History of Seafaring', Thames and
Hudson 1972.
Baynham, Henry, 'Before the Mast-Naval Ratings in the
Nineteenth Century', Hutchinson, 1971, 'Men from the
Dreadnoughts', Hutchinson, 1971.
Bishop, A.S., 'The Rise of a Central Authority for English
Education', Cambridge University Press, 1971.
Birchenough, C., 'History of Elementary Education', University
Tutorial Press, 1925.
Bosanquet, H., 'Rich and Poor', 1898.
Bruce, M., 'The Coming of the Welfare State', Batsford, 1961.
Burn, W.L., 'The Age of Equipoise', Allen & Unwin, 1964.
Chadwick, E.E., 'Report on the Training Systems for the Navy
and the Mercantile Marine of England and France',
Government Printing Office, Washington, USA, 1880.
Curtis, S.J. & Boultwood, M., 'An Introductory History of
English Education since 1800', University Tutorial Press, 1967.
Davies, H.R., 'The Conway and Menai Ferries', University of

Wales Press, Cardiff, 1966.

Dewey, John, 'The School and the Child', Blackie & Son, u/d.

Dodd, A.H., 'A History of Caernarfonshire 1284-1900',
Caernarfonshire Historical Society, 1968. 'The Industrial
Revolution in North Wales', University of Wales Press, 1933.

Ellis, E.L., 'The University College of Wales, Aberystwyth
1872-1972', University of Wales Press, 1972.

Evans, Gwilym, 'The Entrance Scholarship Examination in
Caernarfonshire', Caernarfonshire Historical Society and
Caernarfonshire County Council, 1966.

Evans, Leslie Wynne, 'Studies in Welsh Education', University
of Wales Press, 1974. 'Education in Industrial Wales 1700-1900',
University of Wales Press, 1971.

Graves, J., 'Policy & Progress in Secondary Education 1902-
1942', Nelson, 1943.

Griffith, J.E., 'Pedigrees of Anglesey and Caernarfonshire
Families', Morton & Sons, 1914.

Hole, James, 'Light, More Light, on the present state of
Education amongst the Working Classes of Leeds", Original
edition by Longman Green 1860. Reprinted The Woburn Press,
1969.

Jones, J. Owain, 'The History of the Caernarfonshire
Constabulary 1856-1960', Caernarfonshire Historical Society,
1963.

Leach, R.A., 'Pauper Children – Their Education and Training',
Hadden Best & Co., 1890.

Lewis, Michael, 'The Navy in Transition – A Social History
1814-1864', Hodder & Stoughton, 1965.

Lloyd, Christopher, 'The British Seaman 1200-1860', Collins,
1968.

Lowndes, G.A.N., 'The Silent Social Revolution', Oxford
University Press, 1947.

Maclure, J.S., 'One Hundred Years of London Education 1870-
1970', Allen Lane Penguin Press, 1970. 'Educational

Documents', Methuen, 1973.

Magnus, Philip, 'Gladstone', John Murray, 1963.

Masefield, John, 'The Conway', Heinemann, 1953.

Millington, E.C., 'Seamen in the Making – A Short History of Nautical Training', J.D. Potter, 1935.

Morgan, K.O., 'Wales in British Politics 1868-1922', University of Wales Press, 1970.

Murphy, J., 'The Education Act 1870', David and Charles, Newton Abbot, 1972.

Ryder, J. & Silver, H., 'Modern English Society – History and Structure 1850-1970', Methuen, 1970.

Simon, Brian, 'Studies in the History of Education 1780-1870', Lawrence & Wishart, 1964. 'Education and the Labour Movement 1870-1920', Lawrence & Wishart, 1965.

Thomas, I.D., 'Gwleidyddiaeth Cymru 1850-1900', Gwasg Prifysgol Cymru, 1973.

Thomson, David, 'England in the Nineteenth Century', Pelican Books, 1950.

Tobias, J.J., 'Nineteenth Century Crime: Prevention and Punishment', David and Charles, Newton Abbot, 1972.

Vincent, J.E. (Editor), 'The Memories of Sir Llewelyn Turner', London Ibister & Co. Ltd., 1903.

Williams, E.A., 'Hanes Môn yn y Bedwaredd Ganrif ar Bymtheg', Cymdeithas Eisteddfod Gadeiriol Môn, 1927.

Winton, John, 'Hurrah for the Life of a Sailor', Michael Joseph, 1977.

Articles

Allingham, William, 'Mercantile Marine Education', Shipmasters' Society, Course of Papers, No. 28, October, 1893.

Bosanquet, H.T.A., 'A Training Service for the Mercantile Marine', Journal of the Royal United Service Institution, Vol. XLIX, No. 332, "The Marine Society's Training Ship 'Warspite'", The Nautical Magazine Vol. LXXIV, No. 2,

February, 1905.

Caborne, W.F., 'British Merchant Seamen: Their Training and Treatment', Course of Papers, No. 55, Shipmasters' Society, London, 9th Session, 1898.

Claridge, S.A., 'The First of the County Schools', Caernarfonshire Historical Society Transactions (T.C.H.S.) Vol. 19, 1958.

Eames, Aled, 'Far Tides Calling', Country Quest, Vol. 15, No. 4, October, 1974.

Flynn-Hughes, C., 'Aspects of Poor Law Administration and Policy in Anglesey 1834-1848', Transactions of the Anglesey Antiquarian Society (TAAS), 1950. 'Bangor Workhouse', T.C.H.S. Vol. 5, 1944. 'The Workhouses of Caernarvonshire 1760-1914', T.C.H.S., Vol. 7, 1946.

Jones, G. Penrhyn, 'Some Aspects of the Medical History of Caernarvonshire', T.C.H.S., Vol. 23, 1962.

Jones, Peter Ellis, 'Bathing Facilities in Bangor, 1800 to the present day', T.C.H.S. Vol. 36, 1975. 'The Bangor Local Board of Health 1850-1883', T.C.H.S., No. 37, 1976.

Owen, Gwen, 'The Bangor Typhoid Epidemic of 1882', T.C.H.S., Vol. 26, 1965.

Owen, P.E., 'The Beginnings of the County Schools in Caernarvonshire', T.C.H.S., Vol. 18, 1957.

Thomas, David, 'Henry Archer', T.C.H.S., Vol. 11, 1950.

Webster, J.R., 'The Welsh Intermediate Education Act of 1899', The Welsh History Review IV, No. 3, 1967.

Whale, Derek, 'Clio carried an executioner!' Weekend Echo, 1/2 April 1978.

Williams, H.G., 'Education in Caernarvonshire under the School Boards', Catalogue of exhibition – History of Education in Caernarvonshire, Bangor Normal College, 5-7 May, 1970. Caernarvonshire County Records Service 1970.

Reference Books

'Lemprier'r Classical Dictionary of Proper Names mentioned in Ancient Authors', Routledge & Keegan Paul, 1963.
'Y Bywgraffiadur Cymreig hyd 1940', Anrhydeddus Gymdeithas y Cymmrodorion, 1953.
'Family Health Guide', Readers Digest Assoc. Ltd., 1972.